SALES CAREERS UNVEILED:

Your Guide to Choosing, Launching and Accelerating your B2B Sales Career

Copyright

First Edition

ISBN: 9798876749840

Disclaimer

This book is intended for informational purposes only. The views and opinions expressed within are those of the author and not necessarily those of Kindle Direct Publishing or its affiliates. The content in this book is not intended to be a substitute for professional advice. While every effort has been made to ensure the accuracy of the information presented, the author and publisher cannot be held responsible for any errors or omissions, or for any consequences resulting from the use of this information.

Dedications and Acknowledgements

To my loving parents Jean and Peter, who gave me the best start in life imaginable. And to my father for teaching me that thinking for yourself, and being my own man, is one of the most crucial things to achieve.

Finally, to my wife Sahar – who has cheerfully supported me in my failures and celebrated with me in my triumphs. I love you.

There are too many people who contributed to this book to acknowledge, and most wanted to remain nameless. But you know who you are. Thank you!

Table of Contents

The Role of Patience

- Understanding the value of patience in navigating long sales cycles and client negotiations.
- Techniques for practicing patience in high-pressure sales environments.
- The impact of patience on sustainable sales success.

Courage in Sales

- The necessity of courage in facing rejection and taking risks.
- Examples of courageous actions in sales scenarios.
- Building courage through experience and mindset shifts.

Self-Reliance in the Sales World

- Defining self-reliance in a sales context.
- Balancing teamwork and individual initiative.
- Developing self-reliance skills: self-motivation, accountability, and decision-making.

Are You Suited to Sales? A Self-Assessment

- Guided self-assessment questions to determine personal suitability for a sales career.
- Balancing self-perception with feedback from peers and mentors.
- Understanding and embracing your unique sales style.

Conclusion: Embracing Your Sales Personality

- Summarizing the key traits necessary for success in sales.
- Encouraging self-acceptance and continuous personal development.
- Motivational closing on pursuing a career in sales with authenticity.

Chapter 2: Exploring Sales Roles

Introduction to Sales Roles

- Overview of the sales hierarchy and the importance of understanding different sales roles.
- The journey from entry-level to advanced positions in sales.

Sales Development Representative (SDR)

- Role and responsibilities: Prospecting, lead qualification, and setting the stage for sales engagement.

- Skills required: Persistence, excellent communication skills, and the ability to quickly understand client needs.

- Challenges and rewards: High activity levels and the excitement of opening new opportunities.

Account Executive (AE)

- Role and responsibilities: Managing the full sales cycle, from negotiation to closing deals.

- Skills required: Strong relationship-building abilities, negotiation skills, and strategic thinking.

- Challenges and rewards: The pressure of quotas and the satisfaction of closing major deals.

Pre-Sales Consultant

- Role and responsibilities: Bridging the gap between sales and technical aspects, customizing solutions for client needs.

- Skills required: Technical expertise, problem-solving skills, and the ability to communicate complex ideas clearly.

- Challenges and rewards: The technical complexity of products and the gratification of tailoring solutions that win deals.

Chapter 3: Industries and Size of Company

Navigating B2B Sales Industries

- An overview of the diversity in B2B sales industries.

- How different industries offer unique challenges and opportunities.

Tech/Software Sales

- Nature of the industry: Innovation, rapid technological changes, and complex product offerings.

- Required skills and mindset: Tech understanding, adaptability to change, and solution-oriented sales approaches.

- Industry challenges and opportunities: Keeping pace with technology and leveraging it for sales success.

Manufacturing & Distribution Sales

- Nature of the industry: Tangible products ranging from small components to large machinery and goods.

- Required skills and mindset: Knowledge of manufacturing processes, attention to detail, and long-term relationship building.

- Industry challenges and opportunities: Managing extensive product lines and understanding diverse client applications.

Services Sales

- Nature of the industry: Selling intangible services, from consultancy to IT solutions.

- Required skills and mindset: Consultative selling, deep industry knowledge, and the ability to build trust.

- Industry challenges and opportunities: Differentiating services in a competitive market and building long-term client relationships.

Types of Companies and Choosing the Right Company for Your Sales Career

- Understanding how company type influences your sales career.

- Balancing personal goals with the characteristics of different company types.

Large Corporates

- Characteristics: Structured environments, clear progression paths, and competitive settings.

- Advantages and drawbacks: Access to extensive resources and training but potential limitations in flexibility and innovation.

- Navigating a corporate sales career: Strategies for standing out and succeeding in a corporate environment.

Small and Mid-Market Businesses (SMBs)

- Characteristics: More flexible environments, varied responsibilities, and closer team dynamics.

- Advantages and drawbacks: Greater autonomy and learning opportunities but with resource limitations.

- Thriving in SMB sales: Leveraging the flexibility and breadth of roles for career growth.

Start-Ups

- Characteristics: Dynamic and fast-paced environments with a focus on rapid growth.

- Advantages and drawbacks: Opportunities for significant impact and learning, countered by instability and uncertainty.

- Navigating start-up sales: Embracing the risks and rewards of a start-up sales role.

Chapter 4: A Typical Day in the Life Of...

Introduction to Daily Life in Sales

- Brief overview of the dynamic nature of sales roles.

- The importance of routine and adaptability in sales.

A Day in the Life of a Sales Development Representative (SDR)

- Morning: Prospecting and lead generation strategies.

- Midday: Making calls and sending emails; balancing persistence with professionalism.

- Afternoon: Collaboration with marketing and account executives; learning from feedback.

- Evening: Reflecting on the day's achievements and planning for the next day.

- Personal anecdote: A successful lead generation story.

A Day in the Life of an Account Executive (AE)

- Morning: Reviewing sales targets and preparing for client meetings.

- Midday: Conducting discovery calls and presentations; the art of listening and solution selling.

- Afternoon: Negotiating deals and following up on proposals.

- Evening: Networking and relationship building.

- Personal anecdote: Closing a challenging but rewarding deal.

A Day in the Life of a Pre-Sales Consultant

- Morning: Collaborating with sales teams to understand client needs.

- Midday: Developing custom demonstrations and technical presentations.

- Afternoon: Engaging in client meetings and addressing technical queries.

- Evening: Staying updated with product knowledge and industry trends.

- Personal anecdote: Tailoring a solution that clinched a critical sale.

The Thrill of Success

- The exhilaration of closing a big deal.

- Impact of success on team morale and personal career growth.

- Case study: A significant win and its ripple effect within the company.

Facing Failures and Challenges

- Dealing with rejection and lost deals.

- The importance of resilience and learning from failures.

- Overcoming common obstacles: tough competition, client indecision, and internal challenges.

- Personal story: Turning a significant loss into a learning opportunity.

Chapter 5: How to Have a Brilliant Sales Career

Introduction to a Successful Sales Career

- Overview of what defines a successful sales career, and your own definition of "success".

- The importance of aligning personal goals with professional development.

Talent in Sales: Emotional Intelligence and Self-Awareness

- Understanding Emotional Intelligence (EI) and its impact on sales success.

- Techniques for developing EI and self-awareness in sales contexts.

- Real-world applications of EI in building client relationships and negotiating deals.

Developing Sales Acumen

- Defining sales acumen and its components.

- Strategies for honing sales instincts and understanding market dynamics.

- The role of sales acumen in identifying and capitalizing on opportunities.

Cultivating the Right Attitude for Sales

- Exploring the significance of curiosity, determination, and persistence in sales.

- Methods to cultivate these attitudes and their influence on sales performance.

- Resilience in sales: Overcoming setbacks and maintaining a positive outlook.

The Power of Continual Learning

- Embracing lifelong learning as a key component of a sales career.

- Identifying resources for continual learning: mentorship, courses, and industry knowledge.

- Balancing practical experience with theoretical knowledge.

Managing Your Sales Career Carefully

- Strategies for proactive career management and goal setting.

- Managing career transitions and promotions in the sales field.

- The importance of personal branding and network building in career management.

Developing Key Career Skills

- Coachability in Sales: Embracing feedback and adaptability.

- Business Acumen: Understanding business operations and client needs.

- Project Management: Organisational skills and effective time management in sales.

- Marketing Skills: Leveraging marketing knowledge for sales success.

Political Skills: Gaining visibility with those who can affect your prospects

- Understanding office politics & cultivating political acumen.

- Strategies for career growth.

- Political Complexities and Power Dynamics

- Building a sustainable Network

Conclusion: Creating Your Path in Sales

- Summarizing the key ingredients and skills for a successful sales career.

- Encouraging a personalized approach to career development.

- Making a sales career rewarding and fulfilling.

Chapter 6: The Most Common Career Mistakes B2B Salespeople make ... and How to Avoid Them

Introduction to Common Career Mistakes

- Overview of typical pitfalls in a sales career.

- The importance of awareness, feedback, and proactive management in avoiding these mistakes.

The Pitfalls of Being 'One of the Boys/Girls'

- Risks of over-associating with underperformers or complainers.

- Balancing professional relationships and personal friendships at work.

- Strategies for maintaining a positive, professional network.

Reputation for Partying

- How a partying reputation can impact your professional image.

- Drawing boundaries between personal life and professional conduct.

- Tips for professional networking and socializing.

Consequences of Excessive Drinking

- The impact of excessive drinking on your career and health.

- Understanding the importance of moderation.

- Seeking support if necessary and maintaining professionalism.

Managing Your Reputation and Personal Brand

- The significance of reputation and personal branding in sales.

- Techniques for building and maintaining a positive professional image.

- Regularly auditing your online and offline presence.

Course Correction in Career Decisions

- Recognizing and rectifying poor job or industry choices.

- Being adaptable and open to change.

- Strategies for evaluating and making career shifts.

Financial Patience and Planning

- Understanding the balance in financial aspirations: neither rushing nor delaying success.

- Long-term financial planning and career choices.

- Avoiding the pitfalls of unrealistic financial expectations.

Staying Too Long vs. Leaving Too Soon

- Recognizing when it's time to move on from a role or company.

- The risks of staying in your comfort zone.

- Assessing career moves and readiness for new challenges.

The Importance of Setting Goals

- Setting clear, achievable career goals.

- Regularly reviewing and adjusting goals.

- Aligning goals with personal values and career aspirations.

Managing your Manager

- Why you need their support.

- Avoiding veto.

- Getting them on your side.

Conclusion: Avoiding Career Pitfalls

- Summarizing key strategies to avoid common career mistakes.

- Encouraging proactive career management.

- Learning from mistakes and growing in your sales career.

Chapter 7: Potential Career Paths After 3+ Years in Sales

Advancing to a Senior Sales or Partner Manager Role

- Transitioning to Senior Sales: Steps to prepare for a more advanced sales position.
- Skills Enhancement: Building on existing skills and acquiring new ones for a senior role.
- Networking and Visibility: Increasing your internal visibility and networking for advancement.

Becoming an SDR/Inside Sales Manager

- Role and Responsibilities: Overview of the managerial role and its challenges.
- Leadership Skills: Developing skills necessary for effective team leadership and management.
- Performance Management: Strategies for driving team performance and achieving targets.

Moving into Sales Operations

- Understanding Sales Operations: Role scope and its impact on sales efficiency.
- Analytical Skills: Emphasizing the importance of data analysis and strategic planning.
- Cross-Functional Collaboration: Working with different departments for operational success.

Transitioning to Content Marketing

- Leveraging Sales Experience: Using sales insights to create impactful marketing content.
- Content Strategy and Development: Skills for developing and executing content strategies.
- Digital Marketing Knowledge: Understanding digital platforms and marketing metrics.

Becoming a Customer Success Manager

- Focus on Customer Retention: Shifting from account acquisition to retention.
- Building Long-Term Relationships: Skills for nurturing and growing customer relationships.
- Product Expertise and Consultation: Becoming a product expert to offer valuable customer insights.

Pre-Sales Consultant / Engineer

- Technical Proficiency: Developing the technical know-how relevant to your product/service.

- Consultative Selling: Skills for effective consultation and solution-based selling.
- Working with Sales Teams: Collaborating with sales teams to enhance customer engagement and conversion.

Product Management

- Transition to Product Management: Leveraging sales experience to understand customer needs and product development.
- Cross-Functional Leadership: Collaborating with engineering, design, and marketing teams.
- Market Analysis and Product Strategy: Skills for market research and strategic product positioning.

Sales Training and Development

- Educator Role: Moving into a position focused on training new sales hires.
- Curriculum Development: Creating training materials and programs.
- Mentoring and Coaching: Providing guidance and support to budding sales professionals.

Business Development & Go-to-Market (GTM) Manager

- Strategic Partnerships: Identifying and developing new market opportunities.

- Market Expansion Strategies: Skills for market analysis and expansion planning.
- Relationship Building with Key Stakeholders: Networking and relationship management at a strategic level.

Entrepreneurial Ventures

- Starting Your Own Business: Using sales experience to launch a startup.
- Business Planning and Fundraising: Skills for business planning, pitching, and fundraising.
- Market Entry and Growth Strategies: Approaches for entering new markets and business growth.

CRM Manager

- Understanding CRM Systems and their importance
- Role and Responsibility
- Combining a passion for technology and sales processes

Sales Enablement

- Role and Overview of Sales Enablement
- Sales Enablement Strategies
- Tools and Tech

Conclusion: Charting Your Future in Sales

- Evaluating Personal Strengths and Interests: Assessing personal skills and career aspirations for the right path.
- Seeking Mentorship and Guidance: Importance of mentorship in making a career transition.
- Continuous Learning and Adaptation: Embracing lifelong learning and adaptability for ongoing career development.

Chapter 8 Afterword: Charting Your Path in the World of Sales

Appendix: A Quick Guide to Sales Terminology & Jargon

Foreword From the Author: Why I wrote this book and why you need it now more than ever!

Hello there!

First off, I'm delighted that you've picked up this book. I'm here to chat with you, just like an older friend would, about the rollercoaster ride that is a career in B2B sales. Believe me, it's a ride worth getting on, but it's got its twists and turns.

Before we dive in, let's set the record straight – this book is serious business. You've probably come across sales books filled with gimmicks and platitudes, treating sales as a game rather than a profession. That's not what this is about. Here, I've approached sales with the respect and seriousness it deserves. To truly excel in sales, you need to view and conduct yourself as a professional, and that's the tone we're setting here. This book is a no-nonsense, professional guide, tailored for those who are serious about forging a successful, respectable career in sales. It's about elevating your approach and understanding the real depth of what it means to be a sales professional. On the subject of what this book is not, I'll point out that this is not a sales training book. Its focus is on the non-selling aspects of your career, which (oddly) are more important than selling skills! There are literally thousands of sales training books available, and although I recommend you read sales training books regularly, most are a dreadful waste of time.

I've been where you are now, at the starting line, wondering which path to take. I was lucky, you see. My father was a bit of a legend in sales – he'd seen it all, from the dizzying highs to the challenging lows. Over dinners, when I was growing up, he'd share tales from his days in the field, giving me the inside scoop on what it's really like out there. When I was a little older and out of school I'd travel with him too. These weren't just stories he was sharing with me; they were lessons, a kind of roadmap that helped me navigate my own career in sales.

Without these lessons, I might never have even considered a career in sales. Or worse, I might have dived in headfirst without a clue, making blunders that could've cost me years in time, lost opportunities, and a fair bit of heartache. Trust me, learning things the hard way in sales isn't just tough; it can be a real kick in the teeth.

Now, here's the rub: most people don't have someone like my father to guide them, especially before they've even started their first job. That's why I felt this burning need to write this book. I wanted to pack it with all the wisdom he shared with me, combined with my own experiences and the insights from others in the field. We're talking about over a hundred years of sales experience tucked into these pages for you to benefit from.

Sales is an exhilarating world. It's more than just a job; it's a gateway to experiences you've never imagined. You'll meet fascinating people, understand different cultures, maybe even travel to places you've never heard of. And yes, let's not be coy about it – there's a decent amount of dough to be made too.

But here's the kicker: having a superstar sales career is less about being a slick salesperson and more about being a savvy career navigator. You've got to know the lay of the land, understand the pitfalls, and have the foresight to make smart moves.

We'll explore every key aspect of the sales world. From figuring out if this is the right path for you, to choosing the right job, making a stellar start, and sidestepping those career-ending pitfalls that even the most experienced of us can fall into.

Understanding the significance of sales is crucial, not just for those directly involved in the field, but for anyone who wants to grasp how businesses and the economy function. Sales is the engine of any company and, by extension, the economy. It's the driving force that converts products and services into financial success, fuelling business growth and sustainability. Consider that most businesses fail due to lack of sales.

Without effective sales strategies and teams, even the most innovative products or services would struggle to find their place in the market. Sales professionals are the critical link between a company's offerings and its customers, ensuring that customer needs are met, and value is delivered. This exchange is the heartbeat of market economies, facilitating the flow of goods and services, and driving economic growth. In essence, sales is about creating and nurturing relationships that result in mutual value – for businesses, customers, and the broader economy. It's a complex field that demands a blend of strategic thinking, interpersonal skills, and market understanding. The very fabric of our economic system – from local businesses to global corporations – relies on the effectiveness of its sales functions. Understanding this is key to appreciating the profound impact and importance of sales, and sales professionals like you, in our daily lives and the global economic landscape.

So, grab a coffee, settle in, and let's embark on this journey together. What's written here are universal truths and will work for you whether you're based in Los Angeles, London, or Lahore. By the end of this book, you'll not just be ready to step into the world of

B2B sales; you'll be armed with the know-how to make it a truly rewarding and successful venture.

All the very best,

Johnny

Chapter 1: Identifying Suitability for Success and Happiness in B2B Sales

1.1   Introduction to Personal Suitability in Sales

B2B sales is not just a test of skills and strategies but also a reflection of one's personal characteristics. Sales success goes beyond mere technical know-how and enters the domain of personal values and traits (also known as talent), and developed skills (that can be learned and improved through training and practice). Understanding how these personal characteristics influence success in B2B sales is crucial for anyone looking to excel in their sales career.

In the world of B2B sales, personal traits often act as the foundation upon which professional skills are built. Certain inherent qualities can significantly enhance a salesperson's ability to connect with clients, negotiate deals, and navigate the complex sales landscape. For instance, traits like resilience, empathy, and optimism are invaluable in dealing with the ups and downs typical in sales. These inherent characteristics can set the stage for how a salesperson approaches challenges, forms relationships with clients, and ultimately, how they close deals.

However, it's important to recognize that while inherent traits play a critical role, the power of developed skills cannot be underestimated. The art of sales is also a science that can be learned and refined. Skills like effective communication, strategic planning, and client management are not necessarily innate but can be developed through training, experience, and dedicated practice. These skills are the tools that, when used effectively, can amplify one's natural traits and lead to greater success in sales.

The balance between inherent traits and skills that can be developed is where the magic of sales truly happens. It's about leveraging natural tendencies – such as a propensity for interpersonal connections or a calm demeanour under pressure – and enhancing them with learned skills like active listening, persuasive pitching, and analytical thinking. This combination allows sales professionals to approach their roles with a well-rounded arsenal, ready to tackle the unique challenges that B2B sales present.

I can't finish this section without calling out that there are still myths about who is most suited to a successful and satisfying sales career. So, for the record:

- You do NOT need "a way with words" or the "gift of the gab". Sales is about listening, thinking, and helping others get what they want. It's not about conning or manipulating people.

- It is not a glorified 'get rich quick scheme'. True, the top performers can earn in excess of a million a year. But it takes years of study, dedication, sacrifice, and careful career planning to get there.

- It is not a professional dumping ground for the lazy and stupid. To be very successful requires the focus and detail orientation of a lawyer, the people skills of a diplomat, the business acumen of a CEO, the patience of a saint, and the courage of a sportsman walking out into a hostile stadium alone.

In sum, personal suitability in sales is a blend of who you are and what you can learn. It involves a deep understanding of your inherent traits, a commitment to developing essential sales skills, and the ability to integrate both into your professional persona. As we delve deeper into the key values and skills essential for a career in B2B sales, it becomes evident that success in this field is as much about personal growth as it is about professional development.

1.2 Drive for Success

In the high-stakes world of B2B sales, 'drive for success' is more than a catchphrase; it's a fundamental trait that distinguishes top performers from the rest. This drive is an inner force that propels sales professionals to pursue their goals relentlessly, overcome obstacles, and consistently achieve high performance.

Defining 'Drive for Success' in Sales In the context of sales, drive for success is the relentless pursuit of goals and objectives, both personal and professional. It's the motivation that gets a salesperson up in the morning, ready to tackle challenges head-on. This drive is characterized by a strong desire to achieve results, a deep commitment to personal growth, and an unwavering focus on meeting and exceeding targets. It's not just about making sales but about striving for excellence in every aspect of the sales process.

Manifestation of Drive in Successful Sales Professionals This trait manifests in various ways among successful sales professionals. It can be seen in their proactive approach to seeking new business opportunities, their resilience in the face of rejection, and their tenacity in following up with prospects. Driven salespeople are often goal-oriented, setting high standards for themselves and tirelessly working to surpass them. They view each setback as a learning opportunity and are constantly seeking ways to improve their skills and strategies.

Cultivating a Stronger Drive for Success

Developing a stronger drive for success involves a combination of mindset and action. Setting clear, ambitious, yet achievable goals is a starting point. These goals should be specific, measurable, and time-bound, providing a clear roadmap for what success looks like.

Building a routine that fosters discipline and focus can also enhance one's drive. This might include daily planning, regular review of progress, and setting aside time for skill development.

Staying motivated is crucial. This can be achieved by celebrating small wins, maintaining a positive attitude, and surrounding oneself with motivational influences, whether it's inspirational literature, mentors, or peers who encourage and challenge you.

Finally, cultivating a growth mindset is essential. This means embracing challenges, being open to feedback, and viewing failures not as setbacks but as opportunities to grow and learn.

In conclusion, drive for success is a critical ingredient in the recipe for a flourishing career in sales. It's about having an unwavering commitment to your goals, continuously striving for improvement, and maintaining the resilience and optimism needed to navigate the complex world of B2B sales.

1.3 Integrity in Sales

Integrity in sales is the backbone of building and sustaining trust, a crucial element in forging long-term client relationships. In the competitive realm of B2B sales, where the pressure to meet targets is high, maintaining integrity can be challenging yet is undeniably critical for lasting success.

Building Trust & Credibility with Integrity In sales, integrity goes beyond honesty; it encompasses being ethical, transparent, and reliable in all dealings. This trait is essential in earning the trust of clients. In a landscape where clients are often cautious and skeptical, sales professionals who demonstrate integrity stand out. They build trust by making promises they can keep, providing accurate information, and being upfront about what their product can and cannot do. This trust is the foundation of strong, enduring client relationships, as clients are more likely to do repeat business and refer others to salespeople they trust. Closely related to integrity is credibility. Imagine waiting to board an aircraft and seeing the pilot looking anxious, confused, and wearing a volleyball outfit. How would that make you feel about boarding the flight? That's a crude example of the difference that credibility makes.

Observe businesspeople or civic leaders that give you a feeling that their competent, trustworthy, and experienced. Learn what gives you those feelings and try to apply them to how you look, talk, act, speak, present, etc.

Balancing Sales Targets with Ethical Practices
Achieving sales targets is crucial, but how those targets are met matters equally. Integrity involves striking a balance between ambitious sales goals and ethical practices. It means avoiding shortcuts that compromise ethical standards, such as misrepresenting product capabilities or pressuring clients into making decisions. Instead, successful salespeople with integrity focus on understanding the client's needs and offering solutions that genuinely benefit them, even if it means recommending a lesser sale or acknowledging that a product may not be the right fit.

Developing and Maintaining a Reputation for Integrity A reputation for integrity is built over time and maintained through consistent actions. It starts with setting personal standards of honesty and ethical behavior and adhering to them, regardless of external pressures. Being consistent in your principles in all interactions, both with clients and within your own organization, reinforces a reliable and trustworthy image.

Moreover, being open to admitting mistakes and rectifying them can strengthen your reputation for integrity. This openness not only demonstrates accountability but also humanizes the sales process, fostering deeper client connections.

In essence, integrity in sales is not just an ethical obligation but a strategic advantage. It builds the kind of trust that leads to lasting client relationships, creates a positive personal and professional reputation, and ultimately paves the way for sustainable success in the world of B2B sales.

1.4 The Role of Patience

Patience in sales, often underrated, is a vital trait for successfully managing the complex and sometimes prolonged processes typical in B2B environments. It plays a crucial role in managing long sales cycles, complex client negotiations, and the inevitable ebbs and flows of the sales profession.

Navigating Long Sales Cycles and Negotiations with Patience The B2B sales landscape is characterized by long sales cycles that can span several months or even years. This extended timeline is due to the complexity of deals, the higher stakes involved, and the multiple decision-makers typically part of the buying process. Patience here is key. It allows sales professionals to methodically nurture leads, build relationships, and gradually guide prospects through the sales funnel.

In negotiations, patience becomes a strategic tool. It enables salespeople to listen more attentively, understand client needs deeply, and respond thoughtfully. Rushing through negotiations can lead to misunderstandings or missed opportunities to address client concerns effectively. Patient sales professionals are better positioned to negotiate deals that are beneficial for both their clients and their companies.

Practicing Patience in High-Pressure Environments Sales environments are often high-pressure, with targets and expectations constantly looming. Practicing patience in such settings involves managing your own expectations and reframing how you view the sales process. Recognizing that not every client interaction will lead to an immediate sale and that building trust takes time can alleviate some of the pressures.

Another technique is to focus on the process, not just the outcome. Celebrating small victories, such as a successful client meeting or positive feedback, can instill a sense of progress and patience. Mindfulness practices and stress management techniques can also help maintain a patient and clear-headed approach.

Impact on Sustainable Sales Success Patience contributes significantly to sustainable sales success. It fosters a more thoughtful and client-centric approach, often leading to stronger, trust-based client relationships. This approach not only increases the likelihood of closing deals but also paves the way for future business and referrals.

In essence, patience in sales is about understanding that success is a gradual process. It involves building and nurturing relationships, adapting to client timelines, and maintaining a steady commitment to your goals. This patient approach often leads to more fulfilling and long-lasting business relationships, marking the path for a rewarding career in B2B sales.

1.5 Courage in Sales

Courage, often an overlooked trait in the world of sales, is fundamental in mastering the uncertainties and challenges inherent in this field. It is the driving force that empowers sales professionals to face rejection, take calculated risks, and step out of their comfort zones.

Facing Rejection and Risks with Courage In sales, rejection is a common occurrence. It takes courage to continuously reach out to new prospects, knowing that not every interaction will result in success. This courage is about resilience, the ability to bounce back and continue pushing forward despite setbacks. It's also about not taking rejection personally but viewing it as an integral part of the learning and growth process in sales.

Taking risks is another area where courage plays a crucial role. This might involve exploring new markets, pitching innovative ideas to clients, or changing long-standing sales strategies. Courage in these scenarios is about having the conviction to try something new and the fortitude to bear the uncertainty that comes with it.

Examples of Courageous Actions in Sales
Courageous actions in sales can take various forms. It could be as simple as making a cold call to a high-value prospect or as complex as proposing an unconventional solution to a client's problem. It might involve challenging a client's perspective when you believe there is a better solution to their problem or standing by your product's value proposition in the face of price negotiations.

Building Courage Through Experience and Mindset Shifts
Building courage in the sales field is a gradual process. It often starts with small steps, like pushing yourself to make one more call after a series of rejections. Experience is a great teacher; each

challenging situation faced adds a layer to your courage.

Mindset shifts are also critical in developing courage. This involves shifting focus from fearing failure to valuing growth and learning. Embracing a growth mindset, where challenges are seen as opportunities to improve, can significantly enhance one's courage.

Additionally, seeking feedback and learning from both successes and failures can bolster confidence and, subsequently, courage.

In conclusion, courage in sales is about embracing and overcoming the fears and uncertainties that are part and parcel of the sales profession. It's about the willingness to face rejection, take risks, and continuously strive for growth, making it a key ingredient for long-term success in sales.

1.6 Self-Reliance in the Sales World

In the multifaceted world of sales, self-reliance is a pivotal trait that empowers individuals to navigate the unpredictable and often challenging landscape. In a sales context, self-reliance is about the ability to operate independently, make informed decisions, and take responsibility for one's actions and their outcomes.

Defining Self-Reliance & Self-Discipline in Sales
Self-reliance in sales refers to the capacity of a salesperson to manage their workload, devise strategies, and solve problems without constant guidance. It involves having the confidence and competence to handle various aspects of the sales process, from prospecting to closing deals. A self-reliant sales professional can set goals, create action plans, and proactively seek solutions to challenges they encounter. This trait is crucial in an environment where situations can change rapidly, and the ability to adapt and act decisively often spells the difference between success and failure. This is even more true post-Covid than it has ever been. You will likely spend protracted periods of time working from home and travelling. There will only be you to keep you focused and motivated, and nobody to blame if your shirt gets horribly stained changing your tire before the big meeting and you forgot to pack a spare!

Balancing Teamwork and Individual Initiative
While self-reliance emphasizes individual competence and initiative, it does not negate the importance of teamwork. The key is finding a balance. Effective sales professionals know when to leverage the strengths of their team and when to take the lead. They collaborate and contribute to team objectives while being capable of working independently to

achieve their personal targets. This balance ensures that while they are self-sufficient, they also value and utilise the collective skills and knowledge of their team.

Developing Self-Reliance Skills Building self-reliance in sales involves honing several key skills:

1. **Self-Motivation:** Cultivating an inner drive to achieve goals, even in the absence of external encouragement. This involves setting personal benchmarks for success and finding motivation in one's progress and achievements.

2. **Accountability:** Taking responsibility for one's actions and their results. This means not only celebrating successes but also owning up to and learning from mistakes.

3. **Decision-Making:** Developing the ability to make quick, informed decisions is crucial. This involves analyzing information, weighing pros and cons, and being decisive in taking actions.

Developing self-reliance is a continuous process that evolves with experience. It requires self-awareness, a willingness to learn from each situation, and the resilience to keep moving forward despite setbacks.

In sales, where independence and adaptability are key, self-reliance is an invaluable trait that drives personal and professional growth.

1.7 Are You Suited to Sales? A Self-Assessment

Determining whether one is suited for a career in sales involves introspection and a willingness to objectively assess one's skills and personality traits. It's a blend of self-perception and the valuable insights that can be gleaned from feedback received from peers and mentors.

Balancing Self-Perception with Feedback Self-perception is your own understanding of your capabilities, strengths, and weaknesses. It's crucial to be honest with yourself about your traits and how they align with the demands of a sales career. Do you have the resilience to face rejection? Are you comfortable with the uncertainty and the dynamic nature of sales? Can you effectively communicate and build relationships? Answering these questions requires a high level of self-awareness.

However, self-assessment should not occur in isolation. Feedback from peers, mentors, and managers can provide an external perspective that might reveal strengths and weaknesses you weren't aware of. This feedback can help confirm or challenge your self-perceptions and guide your professional development. For instance, you might perceive yourself as an effective communicator, but feedback could reveal areas for improvement in this skill.

Understanding and Embracing Your Unique Sales Style Every sales professional has a unique style – a combination of personality traits, communication skills, and approaches to selling. Some might excel in building long-term relationships, while others might be adept at quick deal closures. It's important to understand what your style is and how it fits into the broader context of sales.

Are you more consultative, focusing on building trust and providing tailored solutions? Or are you more of a challenger, known for pushing clients to think differently and stepping out of their comfort zones? Embracing your style means leveraging your natural tendencies in a way that aligns with effective sales strategies.

Additionally, it's important to recognize that your unique sales style can evolve. As you gain experience and learn from successes and failures, your approach to sales might shift. Being open to this evolution is part of embracing your journey in sales.

In conclusion, understanding whether you are suited for a career in sales involves a combination of introspection, embracing your unique style, and integrating feedback from others. It's about recognizing your inherent traits, understanding how they align with the demands of a sales role, and being open to continuous learning and adaptation. This self-assessment is a vital step in carving out a successful and fulfilling career in sales.

Here's a list of 15 questions designed for a guided self-assessment to help determine personal suitability for a career in sales:

1. **Resilience Assessment**: When faced with rejection or failure, how quickly do you bounce back and what is your strategy for moving forward?

2. **Communication Skills**: How comfortable and effective are you in communicating, both in speaking and writing, with diverse groups of people?

3. **Relationship Building**: Do you find it easy to build and maintain relationships, and can you provide examples of strong relationships you have built in professional settings?

4. **Goal Orientation**: How often do you set personal and professional goals for yourself, and what is your track record in achieving them?

5. **Adaptability**: Can you provide examples of situations where you successfully adapted to significant changes or unexpected challenges?

6. **Problem-Solving Skills**: How do you approach problem-solving in complex situations, and can you share an instance where your problem-solving skills significantly impacted an outcome?

7. **Drive and Motivation**: What motivates you in your professional life, and how do you sustain motivation during challenging times?

8. **Listening Skills**: How would you rate your active listening skills, and can you give an example of how your listening ability helped in a professional context?

9. **Learning and Development**: How do you approach learning and development, and what steps do you take to continually improve your skills and knowledge?

10. **Negotiation Skills**: Have you been in situations where you had to negotiate, and what was the outcome? What did you learn from the experience?

11. **Customer-Centric Approach**: How would you handle a situation where a customer's needs are challenging to meet?

12. **Team Collaboration**: Describe how you have worked effectively as part of a team. What role do you usually take in a team setting?

13. **Handling Pressure and Stress**: How do you manage high-pressure situations, especially where quick decision-making is required?

14. **Ethical Decision-Making**: Can you recall a time when you had to make a decision in a grey area? How did you handle it?

15. **Personal Branding**: How do you perceive your personal brand, and how have you developed it in your professional or academic life?

These questions are designed to prompt reflection on key attributes and experiences relevant to a sales career. Honest responses can provide insight into one's suitability for a role in sales and highlight areas for potential development.

Conclusion: Embracing Your Sales Personality

As we conclude our exploration into the personal attributes crucial for a successful career in sales, it's evident that certain key traits stand out. Resilience, effective communication, relationship-building, adaptability, goal orientation, and ethical decision-making form the bedrock of a successful sales personality. These traits, combined with a strong drive for success and a customer-centric approach, set the stage for not only achieving targets but also for building a fulfilling career.

There are some additional points to make here: proactivity and creativity. Unlike some other roles, if you follow the same way everyone else (like your competitors) do things, you likely won't win. You have to be willing and able to logically dissect and analyze a situation then apply your creativity and business/sales acumen to find a new and better way of achieving your goal. And you have to be constantly doing this without waiting for someone (like your boss) to tell you. That's how winners win.

Embracing your sales personality involves acknowledging and accepting your unique blend of these traits. It's about understanding your strengths and areas for improvement. Recognize that while some qualities come naturally, others can be developed and honed over time through experience and dedicated personal development efforts.

As you embark or continue on your sales journey, remember that authenticity is your greatest asset. Authenticity builds trust, creates genuine connections, and ultimately drives sustainable success. Your sales personality, with all its nuances, is what will distinguish you in this competitive field.

Stay committed to continuous learning and self-improvement, and embrace each challenge as an opportunity to grow. With resilience, adaptability, and authenticity, you are well-equipped to navigate the dynamic world of sales and carve out your path to success. Remember, the world of sales is as rewarding as it is challenging, and it is your unique personality and approach that will define your journey in it.

Chapter 2: Types of Sales Jobs

2.1 Introduction to Sales Roles

The landscape of sales is vast, marked by a variety of roles that cater to different stages of the sales process and require distinct sets of skills and attributes. Understanding this hierarchy is crucial for anyone embarking on or plotting a career in sales. It's not just about recognizing the titles but about comprehending the unique responsibilities, challenges, and opportunities each role presents.

At the foundation of this hierarchy are the entry-level positions, such as the Sales Development Representative (SDR). These roles are typically the first step into the world of sales. Here, individuals learn the art of prospecting – identifying and reaching out to potential clients. It's a role that demands resilience and effective communication skills, serving as a proving ground for those aspiring to advance in their sales careers.

As one progresses, the role of an Account Executive (AE) comes into play. AEs take over the baton from SDRs, diving into deeper waters of negotiations and deal closures. This role requires a blend of strategic thinking, relationship management, and a keen understanding of customer needs and solutions. It's a role where sales skills are honed, and major business deals are made.

Beyond the AE role, there are advanced positions like the Pre-Sales Consultant. These roles merge sales acumen with technical expertise, focusing on tailoring solutions to meet specific client needs. They are crucial in complex sales environments, especially in industries like technology and manufacturing, where understanding the intricacies of products or services is key to sales success.

Each step in this sales hierarchy is not just a change in job title but a progression in skills, responsibilities, and understanding of the sales process. Starting from the initial outreach to closing deals and managing client relationships, each role plays a vital part in the overall sales ecosystem. Understanding these roles is not only important for individual career growth but also for the effective functioning of the sales team as a whole.

The journey through these roles is marked by continuous learning and adaptation. As the sales landscape evolves with new technologies and changing market dynamics, so do the roles within it. From entry-level positions to senior roles, each step offers unique lessons and opportunities, contributing to a fulfilling and dynamic career in sales. Whether you're just starting out or looking to advance to the next level, understanding this hierarchy and the nuances of each role is key to successfully following the path to success in sales.

2.2 Sales Development Representative (SDR)

The Sales Development Representative (SDR) is a pivotal role in the B2B sales process, often serving as the initial point of contact between a company and its potential customers. This position is crucial for generating new business opportunities and setting the groundwork for successful sales engagements.

Role and Responsibilities An SDR's primary responsibility is prospecting - identifying and reaching out to potential clients who might benefit from the company's products or services. This involves extensive market research to understand and target the right audience. Once potential clients are identified, SDRs engage in lead qualification, determining which prospects have a genuine need and interest, and the financial capacity to purchase the product or service.

The role requires a strategic approach to outreach, often involving a mix of cold calling, emailing, and social media engagement. SDRs craft compelling messages to pique the interest of potential clients and incite a desire to learn more. They are responsible for setting the stage for further sales engagement, usually by scheduling meetings or calls between qualified leads and Account Executives who will then take the sales process forward.

Skills Required To excel as an SDR, persistence is key. The role often involves facing rejection and requires the resilience to continue reaching out to new prospects. Excellent communication skills are essential, both for effectively conveying the value proposition of the product or service and for listening to and understanding the needs and challenges of potential clients.

Moreover, an SDR must be adept at quickly gauging a client's interest and needs. This requires not only a thorough understanding of the company's offerings but also the ability to adapt messaging on the fly to resonate with diverse prospects. Time management and organisational skills are also crucial, as SDRs must juggle multiple tasks and follow-ups efficiently.

Challenges and Rewards Being an SDR can be challenging due to the high level of activity and the persistence required. The role often involves dealing with rejection and the pressure of meeting outreach and qualification targets. However, these challenges are balanced by the excitement and satisfaction of uncovering new opportunities and contributing directly to the company's growth.

There's a thrill in being the first to make contact with a potential client and successfully piquing their interest. For those passionate about sales, the SDR role offers a dynamic and fast-paced environment where every day brings new challenges and opportunities to learn. It's a role that not only lays the foundation for a career in sales but also provides immense satisfaction from driving tangible business results.

2.3 Account Executive (AE)

The Account Executive (AE) is a key player in the sales hierarchy, responsible for steering the sales process towards successful conclusions. This role is critical in transforming leads into valuable clients, managing the full sales cycle from initial negotiation to the closing of deals.

Role and Responsibilities An AE's journey with a potential client begins where the SDR's role ends. Once a lead is qualified and interested, the AE takes over to deepen the engagement (although, depending on the organization, many AE's are responsible for their own prospecting & lead generation. Some companies may not even have an SDR team). This involves understanding the client's specific needs and challenges, presenting tailored solutions, and convincing the client of the value proposition. AEs are involved in crafting and presenting proposals, negotiating terms, and ultimately closing deals.

Managing the full sales cycle requires a deep understanding of both the product or service and the client's business. AEs often conduct detailed needs assessments, aligning their offerings with the client's strategic objectives and pain points. They are also responsible for maintaining and managing client relationships throughout the sales cycle, ensuring a smooth transition from potential to active client.

Skills Required To excel in this role, strong relationship-building abilities are paramount. AEs must be adept at establishing and nurturing connections with clients, building trust and rapport. Negotiation skills are also critical, as AEs often navigate complex discussions to find mutually beneficial solutions.

Strategic thinking is another vital skill for an AE. This involves not just understanding the client's immediate needs, but also foreseeing and planning for long-term engagement opportunities. AEs must be able to think on their feet, adapt their strategies to varying client scenarios, and handle objections effectively.

Challenges and Rewards The role of an AE is both challenging and rewarding. One of the primary challenges is the constant pressure to meet or exceed sales quotas. AEs operate in a target-driven environment where their performance is closely monitored. This can be stressful, particularly in highly competitive markets or during economic downturns.

However, the satisfaction of closing major deals offers a significant counterbalance to these pressures. There's a unique sense of accomplishment in successfully winning the entire sales cycle, from initial contact to final agreement. Closing a major deal not only contributes to the company's bottom line but also bolsters the AE's professional reputation and can open doors to further career advancement. For those with a passion for sales, the role of an AE offers a dynamic and fulfilling career path, filled with opportunities to make a significant impact on their organisation's success.

2.4 Pre-Sales Consultant

In more specialized or technical sales, the Pre-Sales Consultant plays a crucial role, acting as the bridge between the technical nuances of a product or service and the client-focused world of sales. This role is central to not only understanding a client's needs but also translating those needs into effective, customized solutions.

Role and Responsibilities A Pre-Sales Consultant is involved early in the sales cycle and works closely with both the sales team and potential clients. Their primary responsibility is to understand the technical requirements of the client and map these to the features and capabilities of their product or service. This requires a deep dive into understanding the client's business processes, pain points, and the specific challenges they face.

Pre-Sales Consultants are also responsible for conducting product demonstrations and presentations, often tailoring these to highlight how their solution addresses the unique needs of each client. They need to anticipate and effectively address any technical queries or concerns that might arise during these discussions. Additionally, they play a key role in the preparation of proposals, Requests for Proposal (RFP), and tenders, ensuring that the technical specifications and benefits are clearly outlined and aligned with the client's requirements.

Skills Required Technical expertise is the cornerstone of a Pre-Sales Consultant's skill set. They must have an in-depth understanding of their product or service, along with a broad knowledge of the industry and current technological trends. Equally important are strong problem-solving skills, enabling them to devise effective solutions for complex client needs.

Another critical skill is the ability to communicate complex technical ideas in a clear and comprehensible manner. This involves not just speaking the language of technology but also translating it into the language of business benefits and solutions. A Pre-Sales Consultant must be able to bridge the gap between technical features and practical, tangible benefits for the client.

Challenges and Rewards The role of a Pre-Sales Consultant comes with its unique set of challenges. Mastering the technical complexity of products and tailoring solutions to fit diverse client needs requires a blend of expertise, creativity, and adaptability. Keeping up with the rapid pace of technological advancements can also be demanding.

However, the rewards of this role are significant. There is immense gratification in crafting a solution that perfectly aligns with a client's needs and witnessing the realization of a successful sale. The role offers the satisfaction of solving real-world problems and the opportunity to play a pivotal role in securing significant deals. For those with a passion for technology and sales, being a Pre-Sales Consultant offers a challenging yet rewarding career path, where their expertise directly contributes to the success of their organisation and the satisfaction of their clients.

Chapter 3: Industries and Opportunities

3.1 Navigating B2B Sales Industries

The world of B2B sales is as diverse as the industries it encompasses, each offering its own unique set of challenges and opportunities. This diversity is not just a matter of selling different products or services; it reflects the varied landscapes of business operations, client expectations, and market dynamics. Success in these industries requires an understanding that goes beyond the basics of sales techniques; it demands an in-depth appreciation of the specific characteristics and trends of each sector.

In the tech and software industry, for instance, sales professionals face the exhilarating challenge of keeping pace with rapid technological advancements and shifting market trends. Here, success hinges on the ability to not only understand complex technological products but also anticipate how these innovations can solve real-world business problems. This industry is marked by a fast-paced environment and a constant need for learning and adaptation.

Contrastingly, the manufacturing & distribution sector offers a different flavour of sales experience. Here, the focus often shifts to tangible products, ranging from industrial machinery to consumer goods. Sales professionals in this industry need a thorough understanding of production processes, supply chains, and the specific applications of their products. The key to success in manufacturing sales lies in building long-term relationships and a deep knowledge of the technical aspects of the products.

The service industry, which includes sectors like management consultancy, financial services, and IT services, presents yet another distinct sales landscape. Selling intangible services demands a consultative approach, where understanding the client's business and offering tailored solutions becomes paramount. This industry values deep industry knowledge, problem-solving skills, and the ability to build trust and credibility with clients.

Each of these industries offers unique pathways for career growth and specialization. While the fundamentals of sales—such as relationship building, negotiation, and communication—remain constant, the nuances of each industry shape the day-to-day experiences of sales professionals. Understanding these nuances is key to finding the right fit for you and excelling in the diverse world of B2B sales. The ability to adapt to different industry requirements, client needs, and market changes is what sets apart successful sales professionals in the dynamic landscape of B2B sales.

3.2 Tech/Software Sales

The tech/software sales industry is a dynamic and rapidly evolving field, characterized by continuous innovation and technological advancements. This sector demands not only an understanding of complex product offerings but also an ability to adapt swiftly to the ever-changing tech landscape.

Nature of the Industry Tech/software sales are marked by a fast-paced environment where new technologies and software solutions emerge at a dizzying rate. Sales professionals in this field are not just selling a product; they are offering a gateway to innovation and efficiency. These products often have complex functionalities and multiple applications, requiring a deep understanding of both the technology itself and the client's specific needs.

In this industry, the sales cycle can vary significantly. For some products, especially those that are highly specialized or new to the market, the sales process can be lengthy (sometimes a year or more) and involve educating the client about the product's potential impact on their business. In other cases, where products are more established or the technology is widely understood, the sales cycle might be shorter (measured in days or weeks) and more focused on differentiating from competitors.

Required Skills and Mindset Success in tech/software sales requires more than just general sales acumen. A deep understanding of the technology is crucial. Sales professionals must be able to discuss technical aspects confidently and accurately, translating complex technical jargon into tangible business benefits.

Adaptability is another key skill. With technology evolving rapidly, staying abreast of the latest developments, and understanding how they impact clients is essential. This requires a commitment to continuous learning and a keen interest in the tech field.

A solution-oriented sales approach is also vital. In tech/software sales, success often hinges on understanding the client's unique challenges and demonstrating how your product can solve specific problems or improve business processes.

Industry Challenges and Opportunities One of the primary challenges in tech/software sales is keeping pace with technological advancements. Sales professionals must continuously update their knowledge to remain relevant and credible. Another challenge is the high level of competition, with numerous companies often offering similar products.

However, these challenges also present opportunities. The rapid pace of change means that new markets and needs are constantly emerging, offering sales professionals the chance to be at the forefront of technological innovation. Additionally, the complex nature of these products often results in higher-value deals, which can be highly rewarding.

For those with a passion for technology and an ability to adapt quickly, tech/software sales offer an exciting and lucrative career path. It's a field where innovative products and cutting-edge solutions meet the strategic art of sales, providing endless opportunities for growth and success.

3.3 Manufacturing & Distribution Sales

Manufacturing & Distribution sales is a sector characterized by the trade of tangible products, spanning a broad spectrum from small components to large-scale machinery. This industry requires a unique blend of technical knowledge and sales acumen, given the tangible nature of its products and the detailed understanding required for effective sales.

Nature of the Industry The manufacturing sector deals with a vast array of products, each with its own set of features, applications, and market demands. The products can range from generic parts used across various industries to highly specialized machinery designed for specific applications. Sales professionals in this field need to understand not just the products themselves but also how they fit into the broader manufacturing process and the specific needs of each client.

The sales cycle in manufacturing can vary significantly based on the complexity and customization level of the product. For standard products, the sales process might be quicker, focusing on volume and repeat orders. In contrast, sales involving specialized or custom machinery often entail a longer cycle, involving detailed discussions, customization, and sometimes a consultative sales approach.

Required Skills and Mindset A solid understanding of manufacturing processes and the technical aspects of the products is crucial in this field. Sales professionals must be able to discuss technical specifications confidently and understand how different products can integrate into various manufacturing processes.

Attention to detail is another critical skill. Manufacturing products often have specific requirements and tolerances, and understanding these nuances is key to ensuring client satisfaction and repeat business.

Long-term relationship building is also a cornerstone of success in manufacturing sales. Due to the ongoing need for parts and machinery, developing and maintaining strong relationships with clients can lead to repeat business and referrals, which are invaluable in this industry.

Industry Challenges and Opportunities One of the main challenges in manufacturing sales is mastering your knowledge of & promoting extensive product lines and staying knowledgeable about a wide range of products. Additionally, understanding the diverse applications of these products across different client industries can be complex.

However, these challenges also present significant opportunities. The broad range of products and applications means that there are always new markets and clients to explore. Additionally, the tangible nature of the products allows for clear demonstrations of value, which can be very satisfying in the sales process.

For those with a knack for technical details and a passion for building lasting client relationships, manufacturing sales offer a rewarding and diverse career path. It's an industry where deep product knowledge meets strategic client management, offering a unique blend of challenges and opportunities.

3.4 Services Sales

In the world of B2B sales, selling services presents a unique set of challenges and opportunities. Unlike tangible products, services are intangible and often need to be tailored to meet the specific needs of each client. This sector encompasses a wide range of offerings, from management consultancy to IT solutions, each requiring a specialized approach to sales.

Nature of the Industry Services sales is fundamentally about selling expertise, solutions, and outcomes. The intangible nature of services means that clients are often buying a promise of performance, be it improved efficiency, enhanced expertise, or problem-solving capabilities. The sales process in this sector is less about the features and more about the benefits and value that the service brings to the client.

The industry is characterized by its focus on relationships and trust. Since services often require ongoing client engagement, the initial sale is just the beginning of what is typically a long-term relationship. The sales cycle can be complex and prolonged, involving multiple stakeholders and decision-makers.

Required Skills and Mindset Consultative selling is crucial in services sales. This approach involves acting as an advisor to the client, understanding their challenges, and providing solutions that meet their unique needs. Sales professionals must be adept at listening, understanding client requirements, and crafting tailored proposals that articulate the value and return on investment of the service.

Deep industry knowledge is another critical requirement. Sales professionals need to have a thorough understanding of the industry they are operating in, including the latest trends, challenges, and opportunities. This knowledge allows them to speak the client's language and build credibility.

Building trust is paramount. In services sales, clients need to feel confident in the provider's ability to deliver on their promises. Building and maintaining this trust requires consistency, reliability, and a demonstrable track record of success.

Industry Challenges and Opportunities One of the main challenges in services sales is differentiating your offering in a highly competitive market. With many providers often offering similar services, standing out requires a clear value proposition and a strong brand reputation.

However, these challenges also present significant opportunities. Services sales allow for deep client engagement and the development of long-term relationships, which can be highly rewarding. Successful sales professionals in this sector often become trusted advisors to their clients, leading to repeat business and referrals.

For those with strong interpersonal skills, industry expertise, and a consultative approach, services sales offer a dynamic and fulfilling career path. It's an area where strategic relationship building and solution-focused selling come together, offering a unique blend of challenges and rewards.

3.5 Types of Companies and Choosing the Right Company (and Boss) for Your Sales Career

When embarking on a sales career, the type of company you join can significantly shape your professional experience and growth. Understanding how different companies influence your day-to-day life, learning opportunities, and how they are perceived by recruiters is crucial. Equally important is the role of your direct supervisor or boss in shaping your sales experience and career trajectory.

Impact of Company Type on Sales Experience The size and type of company you work for will greatly influence your sales role. In large corporations, sales roles are often more structured with defined processes and larger resources. They provide a sense of stability and often a clear career path, but they might also come with more bureaucracy and less flexibility. These roles can be impressive on a resume, demonstrating your ability to navigate complex structures and processes.

On the other hand, working in a startup or a smaller company offers a more dynamic and versatile sales experience. You're likely to wear multiple hats, have more responsibility, and enjoy a faster-paced environment. These experiences can be very appealing to future employers, showcasing your adaptability, initiative, and breadth of skills.

The Importance of a Good Boss A good boss in sales can be transformative. They not only mentor and guide you but also shape the sales culture you work in. A supportive and knowledgeable boss can enhance your learning, help you develop essential skills, and create an environment where you can thrive and be successful. They play a key role in your job satisfaction and can influence your decision to stay with a company.

Conversely, a bad boss can hinder your professional growth and job satisfaction. A lack of support, poor management skills, or a negative attitude can create a toxic work environment. In such cases, even a good company might not offer a fulfilling experience.

Choosing the Right Company and Boss When considering a job offer, research the company's culture, market reputation, and the specific team you'll be joining. Look for companies and roles that align with your career goals and personal values.

Similarly, during interviews, try to gauge the leadership style and personality of your potential boss. Ask about their management approach, how they support and develop their team, and their expectations.

Remember, it's okay to walk away from an offer if the company or boss doesn't seem right. The wrong fit can be detrimental to your career and well-being in the long run.

In summary, choosing the right company and boss is a crucial decision in your sales career. It's about finding a balance between the opportunities for professional growth, the type of sales culture you want to be part of, and a boss who can positively impact your career journey. Making the right choice can set you on a path to a successful, rewarding, and enriching sales career.

3.6 Large Corporates

In the diverse landscape of B2B sales, working in large corporates embodies a unique experience characterized by structured environments, clear career progression paths, and competitive settings. This sector attracts those who seek stability, resources, and well-defined growth opportunities within the world of sales.

Characteristics of Large Corporates Large corporate environments are marked by their structured approach to business. They often have established processes, protocols, and hierarchies, which provide a clear framework within which sales activities operate. Career paths in these organisations are typically well-defined, offering sales professionals a clear roadmap of the progression opportunities available, from entry-level positions to senior roles.

The competitive nature of these environments cannot be understated. Sales teams in large corporates are often driven by targets and performance metrics, fostering a culture that is both challenging and results-oriented. This setting demands a high level of motivation and a constant drive to achieve and exceed set goals.

Advantages and Drawbacks One of the main advantages of working in large corporates is access to extensive resources and training. These organisations often have the means to invest in comprehensive training programs, state-of-the-art sales tools, and technology, which can be invaluable in developing and honing sales skills.

Moreover, large corporates usually offer substantial support systems, including marketing, research, and administrative assistance, enabling sales professionals to focus more on selling and less on ancillary tasks.

However, these advantages can come with limitations. The structured nature of large corporates can sometimes lead to less flexibility and room for innovation in sales approaches. Sales professionals may find themselves ploughing through more bureaucracy and adhering to stricter protocols than in smaller, more agile organisations.

Navigating a Corporate Sales Career To succeed in a large corporate environment, standing out is key. This involves not only meeting sales targets but also demonstrating a capacity for strategic thinking and leadership. Building a personal brand within the organisation can be crucial. This means being known not just for sales numbers but also for problem-solving abilities, collaboration skills, and innovative thinking.

Networking within the organisation is also vital. Developing relationships across different departments and levels can open up opportunities for mentorship, collaboration, and visibility.

Embracing continuous learning and development is another strategy for success. The best sales professionals in large corporates are those who stay abreast of industry trends, sales methodologies, and technological advancements, continually adding to their skill set.

In summary, a career in sales within large corporates offers a blend of stability, resources, and clear progression paths, balanced with the need for adaptability, strategic thinking, and personal branding. For those who thrive in structured and competitive environments, it presents a robust platform for professional growth and success in sales.

3.7 Small and Mid-Market Businesses (SMBs)

In the diverse ecosystem of sales careers, Small and Mid-Market Businesses (SMBs) offer a distinct and dynamic environment. Characterized by more flexible structures, varied responsibilities, and closer team dynamics, SMBs present unique opportunities and challenges for sales professionals.

Characteristics of SMBs SMBs typically operate with more agility than their larger corporate counterparts. This flexibility often translates into a less hierarchical and more collaborative work environment. Sales roles in these businesses can encompass a broader range of responsibilities, requiring professionals to wear multiple hats. Unlike in larger organisations where roles are highly specialized, sales personnel in SMBs might find themselves involved in various aspects of the business, from client acquisition to account management, and even marketing initiatives.

The team dynamics in SMBs tend to be closer-knit, fostering a sense of camaraderie and mutual support. With smaller teams, individual contributions are more visible and impactful, making each team member's role crucial to the company's success.

Advantages and Drawbacks One of the most significant advantages of working in SMB sales is the opportunity for greater autonomy. Sales professionals often have more freedom to innovate and develop personalized sales strategies. This autonomy encourages creativity and can lead to a more satisfying work experience.

Additionally, the varied responsibilities present in SMBs offer tremendous learning opportunities. Sales professionals can gain a broad skill set and a deeper understanding of the business as a whole, and more time with senior leaders, which can be invaluable in career progression.

However, working in SMBs also comes with its challenges. Resource limitations can be a common issue, with smaller budgets for training, marketing, and sales tools compared to larger companies. This requires sales professionals to be more resourceful and sometimes do more with less.

Thriving in SMB Sales To thrive in SMB sales, embracing the flexibility and variety of roles is key. Sales professionals should take advantage of the opportunity to develop a broad range of skills and deepen their business acumen.

Building strong relationships within the team and contributing to the collaborative culture can also enhance career prospects in SMBs. The close-knit nature of these businesses means that teamwork and interpersonal skills are highly valued.

Additionally, sales professionals in SMBs should focus on developing their ability to work effectively under resource constraints. This involves being innovative in sales approaches, leveraging available tools to the fullest, and continuously seeking ways to optimize processes and strategies.

In conclusion, SMBs offer a dynamic and versatile environment for sales careers, with the potential for significant personal and professional growth. For those who thrive in agile settings and seek a broad, hands-on sales experience, SMBs present an ideal platform for developing a well-rounded sales skill set and an entrepreneurial mindset.

3.8 Start-Ups

In the vibrant landscape of sales careers, start-ups stand out with their dynamic and fast-paced environments. These budding enterprises are defined by their focus on rapid growth and innovation, offering a unique set of experiences for sales professionals.

Characteristics of Start-Ups Start-ups are known for their agility and urgency. In these environments, sales roles are often less about maintaining the status quo and more about driving growth and capturing market share. The pace is quick, the atmosphere charged with energy and a sense of purpose. Here, sales teams are typically on the frontline of business expansion, tasked with not only reaching but often exceeding ambitious targets.

The culture in start-ups is usually one of innovation and experimentation. Sales strategies may evolve rapidly, adapting to market feedback and changing business objectives. This continuous evolution requires sales professionals to be adaptable, proactive, and comfortable with a high degree of ambiguity.

Advantages and Drawbacks One of the primary advantages of working in a start-up is the opportunity to make a significant impact. Sales achievements in start-ups can directly influence the company's trajectory, offering a tangible sense of contribution and accomplishment. Additionally, the fluid nature of start-ups often allows for accelerated learning experiences, with sales professionals exposed to a wide range of tasks and challenges.

However, these opportunities come with their set of drawbacks. Instability and uncertainty are common in start-ups. Market success is not always guaranteed, and business models can shift, sometimes drastically. This environment demands a high tolerance for risk and an ability to thrive under potentially stressful conditions.

Navigating Start-Up Sales To excel in a start-up sales role, embracing both the risks and rewards is essential. Sales professionals need to be comfortable with a certain level of uncertainty and be able to operate effectively even when directions and strategies are in flux.

A key to success in this setting is versatility. Being able to adapt quickly to new products, markets, and sales approaches is critical. Start-ups value professionals who can wear multiple hats and contribute beyond traditional sales roles.

Networking and relationship-building within the start-up community can also be beneficial. Connections made in this ecosystem can open doors to new opportunities and partnerships, which are crucial in the start-up world.

Being proactive about learning and personal development is another important aspect. In the rapidly evolving start-up environment, staying ahead of industry trends and continuously honing sales skills can set a professional apart.

In conclusion, start-ups offer a dynamic and exhilarating environment for sales careers, marked by opportunities for substantial impact and rapid professional growth. For those who are resilient, adaptable, and thrive in high-energy settings, start-ups provide a platform to push boundaries and redefine traditional sales roles.

Chapter 4: The Real World of B2B Sales

4.1 Introduction to Daily Life in Sales

In the world of B2B sales, each day ushers in a unique blend of challenges and opportunities. For those on the front lines of this dynamic profession, the only constant is change. Sales roles, especially in the B2B sector, are far from monotonous. They demand a combination of strategic thinking, adaptability, and a relentless pursuit of goals.

Imagine starting your day with a clear set of targets – calls to make, emails to send, presentations to prepare. Yet, as the day unfolds, so does the realization that each interaction, each client, brings a different set of variables into play. This is the beauty and challenge of a sales role: no two days are alike, and no single approach fits all scenarios. It's a profession that keeps you on your toes, constantly learning, and perpetually growing.

A fundamental aspect of thriving in this environment is establishing a routine. Successful sales professionals often speak about the power of a well-structured day. It's about finding that perfect balance between scheduled activities and the flexibility to adapt to unforeseen opportunities or challenges. A routine might start with reviewing goals and KPIs, followed by a block of time dedicated to prospecting and lead generation. The middle of the day could be reserved for meetings and follow-ups, while the latter part might focus on strategizing for the next day and learning from the day's interactions.

Yet, the importance of adaptability cannot be overstressed. In sales, the ability to pivot, to embrace change, is as crucial as any well-laid plan. It's about being ready to modify your approach based on customer feedback, market trends, or even internal changes within your organisation. This blend of routine and adaptability is what makes a career in sales both challenging and rewarding. It's not just about selling a product or service; it's about traversing a landscape that is constantly evolving, building relationships, and crafting solutions that meet ever-changing needs. This is the daily life of a sales professional – a journey of continual learning and adaptation, set against the backdrop of ambitious targets and the relentless pursuit of success.

4.2 A Day in the Life of a Sales Development Representative (SDR)

Morning: Prospecting and Lead Generation Strategies

The day of a Sales Development Representative (SDR) begins with the cornerstone of sales success – prospecting. In the quiet hours of the morning, I dive into researching potential clients, analyzing market trends, and identifying key decision-makers. This process isn't just about gathering names and email addresses; it's about understanding the needs and pain points of each prospect, tailoring my approach to address their specific challenges. I utilise various tools, from LinkedIn to specialized sales software, to build a list of qualified leads. It's a meticulous task, requiring both patience and strategic insight. Each lead could be the gateway to a significant opportunity, and it's essential to lay the groundwork carefully.

Midday: Making Calls and Sending Emails

As the day progresses, my focus shifts to outreach. Armed with a list of carefully curated leads, I begin the process of making calls and sending emails. This is where persistence meets finesse. Each call is an opportunity to connect, to introduce our solutions, and to gauge the interest of potential clients. I'm mindful of the fine line between being persuasive and being intrusive. It's a skill that I've honed over time – learning how to read the tone of a conversation, when to push forward, and when to step back. My emails follow a similar philosophy; they are concise, personalized, and always value-driven. I aim to start a conversation, to pique interest, and to set the stage for a deeper engagement by our account executives.

Afternoon: Collaboration with Marketing and Account Executives

The afternoon is often the most collaborative part of my day. I meet with our marketing team to discuss the effectiveness of our current strategies and to explore new ways to engage our target audience. These sessions are invaluable; they provide insights into broader market trends and help refine our messaging. I also spend time with account executives, passing along qualified leads and sharing insights I've gathered during my morning prospecting. These interactions are crucial – they ensure a seamless transition from initial contact to deeper engagement. It's a symbiotic relationship; the success of our account executives is directly tied to the quality of leads I provide. Learning from their feedback, understanding the nuances of each potential deal, helps me refine my approach to prospecting.

Evening: Reflecting on the Day's Achievements and Planning for the Next Day

As the day winds down, I take time to reflect on my achievements and the lessons learned. This quiet hour of contemplation is crucial for my professional growth. I review the conversations I've had, analyze the responses to my emails, and assess the progress made with each lead. It's a time to celebrate the small victories – a positive response, a scheduled meeting – and to learn from the less successful encounters. This reflection helps me plan for the next day, setting clear goals and strategies. It's a continuous cycle of action, assessment, and adjustment, each step building upon the last.

Personal Anecdote: A Successful Lead Generation Story

I recall a particularly challenging lead, a prospect in a highly competitive industry that had eluded engagement despite repeated attempts. The breakthrough came not through persistence, but through a creative approach. I noticed the prospect was active in an industry forum online, often discussing challenges unique to their business. Instead of another call or email, I crafted a detailed report addressing one of these challenges, highlighting how our solution could be tailored to meet their specific needs. I sent this along with a personalized note, acknowledging their expertise and offering insights without any overt sales pitch. The response was more than I could have hoped for; not only did it lead to a meeting, but it also opened doors to a level of engagement we hadn't managed with this company before. This experience was a testament to the power of understanding and addressing a prospect's unique needs, and it has since shaped my approach to lead generation.

4.3 A Day in the Life of an Account Executive (AE)

Morning: Reviewing Sales Targets and Preparing for Client Meetings

As an Account Executive (AE), my day begins with a strategic overview. I start by reviewing my sales targets, aligning them with my daily and weekly goals. This ritual sets the tone and pace for the day ahead. Attention then shifts to preparing for client meetings. Preparation is key; it involves not just reviewing notes or presentation slides but also delving into the client's background, their industry trends, and potential pain points. This process ensures that I'm not just ready to talk but, more importantly, ready to listen and understand the client's needs. I rehearse my pitch, anticipate questions, and plan for different scenarios. This thorough preparation underscores my commitment to not just meeting but exceeding client expectations.

Midday: Conducting Discovery Calls and Presentations

As the day progresses, I engage in the core of my role – discovery calls and presentations. Each call is an opportunity to delve deeper into the client's world, uncovering their needs and challenges. The art of listening is crucial here; it's about understanding not just what is said, but also what is left unsaid. I strive to build a rapport with each client, ensuring they feel heard and understood. Presentations are tailored to each client, focusing on how our solutions can specifically address their unique challenges. This is solution selling at its best – consultative, personalized, and client-focused. It's a balancing act of being persuasive yet receptive, assertive yet accommodating.

Afternoon: Negotiating Deals and Following Up on Proposals

Post-lunch, my focus shifts to negotiations and follow-ups. Negotiating deals is a nuanced dance; it requires a deep understanding of the client's constraints and preferences, and the ability to find a mutually beneficial middle ground. I juggle various negotiations, keeping track of details, and making sure each party feels valued and respected. Following up on proposals is equally important. It involves reaching out to clients who have received our proposals, addressing any concerns, and reinforcing the value we offer. This phase is critical as it often determines whether a deal moves forward or stalls.

Evening: Networking and Relationship Building

As evening approaches, my role extends beyond the immediate sales tasks to networking and relationship building. Whether it's attending industry events, joining online webinars, or informal catch-ups with clients and peers, each interaction is an opportunity to strengthen professional relationships. Networking is an integral part of being an AE; it's about cultivating a broad and diverse network that can open doors to new opportunities and insights. This time is also used for nurturing existing relationships, checking in with long-term clients, and staying connected with key contacts.

Personal Anecdote: Closing a Challenging but Rewarding Deal

One of my most memorable deals was with a client who was initially skeptical about our solution's applicability to their complex needs. The deal took months of discussions, presentations, and negotiations. I remember the turning point was during a tailored presentation where we addressed each of their concerns in detail, demonstrating a deep understanding of their industry and challenges. The client's demeanour changed from scepticism to interest, and eventually to trust. What made this deal particularly rewarding was not just its size but the journey it entailed – from overcoming initial reluctance to building a relationship based on mutual respect and understanding. Closing this deal was a testament to persistence, adaptability, and the importance of truly understanding and addressing client needs. It was a deal that not only brought significant revenue but also deepened my learning and growth as a sales professional.

4.4 A Day in the Life of a Pre-Sales Consultant

Morning: Collaborating with Sales Teams to Understand Client Needs

My day as a Pre-Sales Consultant starts with collaboration. I meet with the sales teams to discuss new leads and ongoing opportunities. These meetings are crucial for aligning our strategies – while they bring insights from client interactions, I contribute technical knowledge and solution design expertise. Together, we review client profiles, dissecting their business environments, challenges, and specific needs. This collaboration is not just about imparting technical information; it's about crafting a narrative where our solutions seamlessly fit into the client's world. Every detail, from the client's industry jargon to their unique business processes, is considered to ensure our approach is both relevant and compelling.

Midday: Developing Custom Demonstrations and Technical Presentations

With a clear understanding of the client's needs, I dedicate the middle part of my day to developing custom demonstrations and technical presentations. This process involves more than just showcasing our product's features; it's about creating a story where the client sees their problem being solved. I delve into each feature, tweaking and adjusting to align with the client's specific scenario. This is where my technical expertise intersects with creativity – simulating real-world scenarios, anticipating potential objections, and highlighting unique selling points. The goal is to make each demonstration not just informative but also engaging, making the complex seem approachable and the technical feel intuitive.

Afternoon: Engaging in Client Meetings and Addressing Technical Queries

Afternoons are often the most client-intensive part of my day. I join the sales team in meetings, presenting our solutions and addressing technical queries. This is where the groundwork of the morning and midday comes to life. As I present, I focus on clarity and relevance, ensuring that the technical aspects are easily understandable. Addressing client queries is where I shine – clarifying doubts, offering insights, and sometimes, even improvising solutions on the spot. These interactions are not just about technical validation; they're about building trust and confidence in our solution's ability to address the client's specific needs.

Evening: Staying Updated with Product Knowledge and Industry Trends

The world of technology is ever evolving, and staying updated is not just an option but a necessity. In the evenings, I dedicate time to expanding my knowledge – studying new product updates, exploring emerging technologies, and keeping abreast of industry trends. This self-imposed curriculum is vital to my role as a Pre-Sales Consultant. It ensures that I am not just aware of what our products can do but also understand where they stand in the broader technology landscape. This knowledge is crucial for not just client interactions but also for contributing to product development and strategy within our own organisation.

Personal Anecdote: Tailoring a Solution that Clinched a Critical Sale

One of my most gratifying experiences as a Pre-Sales Consultant involved a client in the healthcare industry. They were evaluating our solution against a major competitor. The deal was significant, but more than that, it was technically challenging. The client had a unique set of requirements, and our standard solution didn't fully address these. Recognizing the opportunity and the challenge, I worked closely with our product and engineering teams to tailor a solution. This involved not just customizing existing features but also conceptualizing a new functionality that could be pivotal for the client. After intense sessions of development and testing, we presented this customized solution. The client was not just impressed by the functionality but also by our commitment to meet their unique needs. This level of customization and rapid deployment was something our competitor couldn't match. We clinched the deal, and it marked a significant win not just in terms of revenue but also in demonstrating our ability to innovate and personalize solutions at a rapid pace.

4.5 The Ups and Downs

The Thrill of Success The euphoria of closing a big deal in B2B sales is incomparable. It's a moment that justifies all the hard work, persistence, and strategic thinking that goes into the sales process. This triumph isn't just about numbers on a spreadsheet; it's a validation of the salesperson's skills, the product's value, and the company's market position.

Exhilaration of Closing a Big Deal The moment when a major deal is sealed is often accompanied by an adrenaline rush. It's a mix of relief, pride, and accomplishment. There's a tangible excitement in the air, a sense of having conquered a mountain. This feeling is particularly potent in B2B sales, where deals often involve complex negotiations and long sales cycles. The satisfaction derived from successfully succeeding through these challenges is immense.

Impact on Team Morale and Personal Career Growth A big win has a ripple effect that goes beyond personal success. It significantly boosts team morale. Team members feel a collective sense of achievement and are motivated to pursue their goals with renewed vigour. For the salesperson responsible, such a win is a career milestone. It not only brings recognition from peers and superiors but also opens doors to new opportunities and advancements. It's a testament to their capability and a building block for their professional reputation.

Case Study: A Significant Win and Its Ripple Effect Consider the case of a mid-sized tech company that landed a large contract with a government agency. This deal was not just about immediate financial gain; it positioned the company as a credible player in a highly competitive market. The success brought about a renewed sense of confidence within the team. It led to an increase in investment in R&D and marketing, paving the way for more innovative products and aggressive market penetration. The sales team, buoyed by this victory, adopted more ambitious strategies, setting the stage for sustained growth and success.

4.6 Facing Failures and Challenges

On the flip side of success in sales is the reality of facing failures and challenges. Rejection and lost deals are part and parcel of the sales journey. These setbacks, while disheartening, are valuable learning experiences.

Dealing with Rejection and Lost Deals Rejection, whether it comes in the form of a declined proposal or a lost deal to a competitor, can be tough. It can lead to self-doubt and waning motivation. However, the key lies in how one responds to these setbacks. Successful salespeople view rejections as opportunities to learn and grow. They analyze what went wrong, seek feedback, and refine their approach. This resilience turns potential negatives into powerful lessons.

The Importance of Resilience and Learning from Failures Resilience in the face of failure is a hallmark of successful sales professionals. It involves maintaining a positive outlook, learning from each experience, and not being deterred by setbacks. This resilience is bolstered by a commitment to continuous improvement – be it enhancing product knowledge, refining sales strategies, or improving communication skills.

Overcoming Common Obstacles Sales professionals routinely face challenges like fierce competition, client indecision, and internal hurdles. Overcoming these requires a combination of strategic thinking, adaptability, and persistence. It's about understanding the client's perspective, guiding them past their indecision, and outshining the competition through superior value proposition and relationship building.

Personal Story: Turning a Significant Loss into a Learning Opportunity I recall a particularly challenging period when I lost a substantial deal to a competitor. The initial disappointment was overwhelming. However, upon reflection, I realized that this loss highlighted several areas for improvement in our approach. We had underestimated the competitor's offerings and overestimated our understanding of the client's needs. This realization led to a revamp of our market analysis methods and a more client-centric approach to sales. We also increased our focus on post-sales support, understanding that our relationship with clients shouldn't end with a closed deal. This loss, painful as it was, became a turning point, leading to significant improvements in our sales strategy and customer relationships.

Chapter 5: How to Have a Brilliant Sales Career

5.1 Introduction to a Successful Sales Career

A successful sales career is often perceived as one marked by impressive sales figures and a consistent track record of meeting and exceeding targets. However, true success in sales extends far beyond these metrics. It encompasses a holistic blend of professional achievements, personal fulfillment, and continuous growth. This broader definition recognizes that success is not just about what you accomplish, but also about how you grow and the values you uphold along the way.

At the core of a successful sales career is the alignment of personal goals with professional development. This alignment is crucial because it ensures that your career trajectory not only advances your professional aspirations but also resonates with your personal values and life objectives. It's about finding purpose and satisfaction in your work, whether that's through building meaningful client relationships, contributing to the growth of your company, or developing your skills and expertise in the field.

A successful sales career is also marked by adaptability and resilience. The sales landscape is ever-changing, with new challenges and opportunities constantly arising. Thriving in this dynamic environment requires an ability to learn and adapt, not just in terms of sales techniques and strategies, but also in how you manage your career progression and personal development.

In essence, a successful sales career is a journey that combines achieving sales goals with personal growth, adaptability, and adherence to core values. It's a path where professional accomplishments are in harmony with personal development, leading to not just a successful career but a fulfilling one. But, one of the most important points is that YOU need to define what "success" means. Not everyone wants (or should try to be) the corporate Chief Sales Officer, or even move into sales management. It's about working out what YOU want YOUR career to look like. Also, understand that this WILL change over time as you get older, wiser, and more experienced – so every few years, or following a major life event, ask yourself again what it is you truly want.

5.2 Talent in Sales: Emotional Intelligence and Self-Awareness

In the multifaceted world of sales, Emotional Intelligence (EI) and self-awareness are increasingly recognized as key drivers of success. Unlike traditional views of talent that prioritize aggressiveness and persistence, EI offers a more nuanced understanding of the interpersonal dynamics crucial in sales.

Understanding EI and Self-Awareness in Sales
Emotional Intelligence in sales refers to the ability to understand, use, and manage your own emotions in positive ways to relieve stress, communicate effectively, empathize with others, and defuse conflict. It involves four core skills: self-awareness, self-management, social awareness, and relationship management. Self-awareness, in this context, is the ability to accurately perceive your emotions and understand your tendencies across different sales situations.

Developing EI and Self-Awareness Developing EI and self-awareness starts with introspection. Reflecting on your interactions with clients and colleagues can offer insights into your emotional responses and triggers. Practicing mindfulness and paying attention to your thoughts and feelings can enhance self-awareness.

Another key technique is seeking feedback. Understanding how others perceive your interactions can provide valuable perspectives that you might overlook. Tools like personality assessments can also be useful in gaining deeper insights into your emotional tendencies.

Real-World Applications in Sales In client relationships, EI and self-awareness manifest as the ability to read a client's mood and adapt your approach accordingly. For instance, a salesperson with high EI can sense a client's hesitation or unspoken concerns and address them effectively, thereby building trust and rapport.

During negotiations, EI plays a critical role in understanding and managing both your emotions and those of the client. It enables you to remain calm under pressure, understand the emotional undercurrents of the negotiation, and respond in a way that advances the deal while maintaining a positive relationship.

In conclusion, Emotional Intelligence and self-awareness are invaluable assets in sales. They enhance your ability to connect with clients, navigate the complexities of sales interactions, and ultimately contribute to more effective and successful outcomes. Developing these skills can lead to deeper client relationships, more successful negotiations, and a more rewarding sales career.

An anecdote my father often told me was when he was working for Texaco in the 1970's in his early career. He had a good relationship with his boss, who had been encouraging my father to spend more time in regional office. My father pointed out that he might be sacrificing revenue for the company. At that point the boss looked my father square in the eye, and said "don't EVER make the mistake of thinking that being good at your job is enough to get ahead". Despite being raised on this tale, and seeing how true it is countless times with my own eyes, it's still a mistake I made too many times. Please don't make the same mistake.

5.3 Developing Sales Acumen

Sales acumen is a multifaceted skill set that embodies a salesperson's ability to effectively navigate the selling process. It's not just about knowing the product or service inside out; it's about understanding how to align this knowledge with customer needs, market trends, and sales strategies. Essentially, sales acumen is the keenness and quickness in understanding and dealing with a sales situation in a manner that is likely to lead to a good outcome.

Components of Sales Acumen Sales acumen comprises several key components:

1. **Market Insight**: Understanding the dynamics of the market in which you are selling, including customer behaviors, competitor actions, and industry trends.

2. **Customer Understanding**: The ability to empathize with and accurately assess the needs, challenges, and motivations of customers.

3. **Strategic Thinking**: Applying foresight and planning in sales approaches, considering both short-term gains and long-term relationships.

4. **Solution Framing**: Skilfully positioning your product or service as the solution to the customer's specific problems or needs.

Strategies for Honing Sales Instincts Developing sales instincts involves a combination of experience, observation, and continuous learning. One effective strategy is to regularly engage with customers and actively listen to their feedback. This direct interaction is invaluable in gaining insights into their needs and preferences.

Staying informed about industry trends and competitor movements is another crucial strategy.

This can be achieved through regular reading, attending industry events, and engaging in professional networks. Being well-informed allows you to anticipate market changes and adapt your sales strategies accordingly.

Participating in sales training and workshops can also sharpen your sales acumen. These programs often provide new perspectives and strategies that you can integrate into your sales approach.

Role in Identifying and Capitalizing on Opportunities A well-developed sales acumen plays a critical role in identifying and capitalizing on sales opportunities. With an in-depth understanding of the market and customer needs, you can more effectively identify potential leads and tailor your sales pitch to address their unique challenges.

Moreover, strong sales acumen enables you to anticipate and overcome objections, present solutions more persuasively, and close deals more successfully. In essence, it's about having the right combination of knowledge, insight, and skill to not only recognize opportunities but to turn them into successful sales outcomes.

5.4 Cultivating the Right Attitude for Sales

In the dynamic and often challenging world of sales, the right attitude can make a significant difference in performance and success. Key attitudes such as curiosity, determination, and persistence, alongside resilience, are essential traits for any sales professional.

The Significance of Curiosity, Determination, and Persistence Curiosity in sales manifests as a genuine interest in understanding clients' needs, market trends, and new sales techniques. It drives sales professionals to ask insightful questions, delve deeper into clients' problems, and seek innovative solutions. This trait keeps the sales process fresh and engaging, allowing for a deeper connection with clients and a better understanding of how to serve them effectively.

Determination in sales is the unwavering commitment to achieve goals despite challenges and obstacles. It's about setting targets and doggedly pursuing them, maintaining focus and drive even when faced with difficulties. This attitude is crucial in winning the competitive nature of sales, where perseverance can often be the key to breaking through barriers to success.

Persistence is closely linked to determination but focuses more on the consistent effort over time. It's about not giving up after a rejection or a lost sale but rather continuing to reach out to new prospects and following up with existing leads. Persistence is essential in sales as it often takes multiple interactions to convert a prospect into a client.

Cultivating These Attitudes Developing these attitudes begins with mindset training. For curiosity, it involves fostering a mindset of continuous learning and exploration. This could mean staying updated with industry news, attending workshops, or simply being open to new experiences and ideas.

For determination and persistence, goal setting plays a pivotal role. Setting clear, achievable, and measurable goals can provide direction and motivation. Visualizing success and keeping track of progress can also help maintain determination and persistence.

Another method is through exposure to challenging situations. Stepping out of your comfort zone and taking on challenging tasks can build determination and persistence. Over time, these challenges become less daunting, reinforcing a resilient attitude.

Resilience in Sales Resilience is the ability to bounce back from setbacks and maintain a positive outlook. It's about viewing failures as learning opportunities and not letting them diminish your enthusiasm and confidence. Building resilience can involve reflective practices like journaling, seeking constructive feedback, and maintaining a supportive network.

Resilience also means taking care of your mental and emotional well-being. Activities like exercise, meditation, or engaging in hobbies can help maintain a balanced perspective, contributing to overall resilience in the face of sales pressures.

In conclusion, cultivating the right attitude in sales – curiosity, determination, persistence, and resilience – is integral to success. These attitudes not only positively influence sales performance but also contribute to a more satisfying and sustainable career in sales.

5.5 The Power of Continual Learning

In the ever-evolving landscape of sales, continual learning emerges as a crucial component for long-term success and career progression. In a field driven by changing market trends, evolving customer needs, and advancing technologies, staying informed and skilled is not just an advantage, but a necessity.

Embracing Lifelong Learning in Sales Lifelong learning in sales is about maintaining a growth mindset and being open to new ideas, strategies, and technologies. It's recognizing that the learning journey doesn't end with initial training or the first few years on the job. Instead, it is an ongoing process that keeps a sales professional relevant, competitive, and effective. This commitment to learning not only enhances one's ability to connect with diverse clients and navigate complex sales scenarios but also fosters personal growth and adaptability.

Identifying Resources for Continual Learning To engage in continual learning, sales professionals can tap into various resources:

- **Mentorship**: Learning from experienced mentors in the field can provide valuable insights that aren't found in textbooks. Mentors offer real-world advice, feedback, and can guide on practical approaches to sales challenges.

- **Courses and Training**: With a plethora of online courses, workshops, and seminars available, sales professionals can continually upgrade their skills. Focusing on courses that cover the latest sales methodologies, digital tools, and customer relationship management strategies can be particularly beneficial.

- **Industry Knowledge**: Staying abreast of industry trends, market analysis, and competitor strategies is crucial. This can be achieved through reading industry publications, attending webinars, and participating in trade shows and conferences.

- **Reading**: There are some superb books on sales, business, business skills, and self-development that you must read, study, and implement. Reading enables you to learn from others and benefit from their wisdom and avoid their mistakes. Don't be an idiot and reinvent the wheel. Reading also helps keep you focused and motivated. It gives you new ideas to try, and to leverage in standing out to leaders in your company.

Unfortunately, most business books are a waste of time – particularly sales books. Often they're regurgitated common practice, out of date, inapplicable to your field, etc. The trick is to look for books that have stood the test of time (like SPIN selling by Neil Rackham) or with strong reviews online. Another key point is to always adapt what you read to your own situation and style.

A tip I've really benefitted from is to fit this reading into your 'dead time', that is time when your doing a mindless activity and could use it to multi-task.

For example, when your brushing your teeth, sit down and read a few pages. Or when your in the car listen to the audio book equivalent. Also, whenever possible, make notes, and highlight key sections – you'll better retain the information. Also, when you re-read the book (which you should often with the good ones) you'll be able to go straight to these higher value sections.

- **Balancing Practical Experience with Theoretical Knowledge** While theoretical knowledge is essential, it must be balanced with practical experience. Applying what is learned in real-world scenarios is where true skill development occurs. It's about taking theories and concepts learned through courses and mentorship and testing them in actual sales situations. Reflecting on these experiences, understanding what works and what doesn't, and then adapting strategies accordingly is key to this balance.

In essence, the power of continual learning in sales lies in its ability to keep professionals agile, knowledgeable, and ahead of the curve. By embracing lifelong learning, sales professionals not only enhance their immediate performance but also pave the way for continued success and career growth.

5.6 Managing Your Sales Career Carefully

In the dynamic world of sales, careful career management is as important as meeting your immediate sales targets. It involves strategically planning your career path, setting achievable goals, and building a personal brand and network that supports your growth and transitions.

Strategies for Proactive Career Management and Goal Setting Effective career management in sales starts with setting clear, realistic, and measurable goals. These goals should not only be about hitting sales targets but also about professional development, such as acquiring new skills, earning certifications, or expanding your industry knowledge. It's crucial to break these goals into short-term and long-term objectives and regularly review and adjust them as needed.

Proactive career management also means staying informed about industry trends and future opportunities. This could involve subscribing to industry publications, joining professional associations, or attending workshops and conferences. Keeping an eye on the future helps in aligning your current goals with where you want to be in the next five to ten years.

Mastering Career Transitions and Promotions Transitioning to new roles or seeking promotions in sales requires careful planning and preparation. This might involve taking on additional responsibilities in your current role to gain the necessary experience, seeking out mentorship or coaching to prepare for higher-level positions, or even pursuing further education or specialized training.

It's also important to communicate your career aspirations with your supervisors and HR department. Regular discussions about your career path and goals can open up opportunities for advancement within your organisation.

Networking plays a crucial role in successful transitions. Building relationships with individuals both within and outside your organisation can provide insights into new opportunities and valuable support during transitions.

The Importance of Personal Branding and Network Building Personal branding is about how you market yourself professionally. It's a combination of your expertise, experiences, and the value you bring to the table. Developing a strong personal brand in sales can set you apart and make you more visible to potential employers or clients.

Building your brand involves consistently demonstrating your skills and values in your work, as well as through public forums such as LinkedIn, industry conferences, or blogging. It's about creating a narrative around your professional life that highlights your strengths and successes.

Networking is an extension of your personal brand. It's not just about collecting business cards but building meaningful relationships with people who can influence your career. This includes colleagues, industry peers, mentors, and even clients. Networking can lead to new job opportunities, sales leads, and partnerships.

Effective network building means being genuinely interested in other people, offering help when you can, and keeping in touch regularly. Remember, a strong network is a two-way street; it's as much about what you can offer as what you can gain.

In summary, managing your sales career carefully is about setting strategic goals, being prepared for transitions, and building a robust personal brand and network. It requires a proactive approach, where you are constantly looking ahead and positioning yourself for the next step in your career. With careful planning and consistent effort, you can forge a successful path in the world of sales.

5.7 Developing & Nurturing Key Career Skills

In the competitive field of sales, certain key skills set top performers apart. These skills - coachability, business acumen, project management, and digital marketing - are critical in succeeding in today's complex sales environment.

Coachability in Sales 'Coachability' refers to a salesperson's ability to absorb, process, and apply feedback to improve their selling style and strategies. It's a blend of humility, willingness to learn, and adaptability. Coachable sales professionals are open to constructive criticism and view feedback as an opportunity for growth rather than a personal affront.

Embracing coachability begins with actively seeking feedback from managers, mentors, or peers. This involves listening attentively, asking clarifying questions, and demonstrating a genuine commitment to applying the feedback. It also means being open to continuous learning, whether through formal training, observing others, or self-reflection.

A coachable salesperson is quick to adapt their strategies based on feedback. This might mean altering their communication style to better connect with clients or tweaking their sales pitch to address previously overlooked client needs. The key is flexibility and a constant pursuit of improvement, essential in an ever-evolving sales landscape.

Business Acumen Business acumen in sales involves understanding not just your product or service, but also how it fits into the broader context of your client's operations and industry. It's about comprehending the economic forces, market dynamics, and business processes that influence purchasing decisions.

Developing business acumen requires staying informed about industry trends, market conditions, and your clients' business models. This can be achieved through regular reading of industry publications, attending business workshops, and engaging in conversations with clients about their challenges and objectives.

Applying business acumen in sales means being able to speak the language of business. It's about articulating how your product or service can impact a client's bottom line, improve efficiency, or give them a competitive edge. Sales professionals with strong business acumen can bridge the gap between a client's needs and their company's offerings, leading to more meaningful and successful sales engagements.

Project Management Effective project management skills are crucial in sales for organizing and executing sales plans, managing multiple clients, and meeting targets. It involves setting clear objectives, planning, prioritizing tasks, and monitoring progress.

Organisational skills are key to managing the various elements of the sales process. This includes keeping track of client interactions, managing sales pipelines, and ensuring that all sales activities are aligned with broader sales goals.

Time management is another critical aspect of project management in sales. Sales professionals must juggle various tasks, from prospecting and client meetings to administrative work and training. Effective time management involves prioritizing tasks based on their impact on sales goals and making efficient use of available time.

Incorporating project management tools and techniques can greatly enhance efficiency and effectiveness in sales. Utilizing customer relationship management (CRM) systems, setting regular check-ins for goal progress, and employing time-management methodologies can help keep sales efforts organized and on track.

Digital Marketing Skills In today's digital age, sales professionals benefit greatly from possessing digital marketing skills. Understanding demand generation and lead generation tactics can significantly enhance a salesperson's ability to identify and capture potential sales opportunities.

Developing digital marketing skills involves learning about various online platforms and tools used in marketing campaigns. This includes understanding social media marketing, content marketing, search engine optimization (SEO), and email marketing.

A key aspect of leveraging digital marketing in sales is aligning sales strategies with marketing efforts. This can involve collaborating with the marketing team to ensure consistent messaging, using marketing materials effectively in the sales process, and understanding how to nurture leads generated through digital marketing channels.

Digital marketing also involves analyzing data to understand customer behaviors and preferences. Sales professionals with digital marketing skills can interpret this data to tailor their sales strategies, personalize their approach, and increase their chances of closing deals.

In conclusion, developing these key career skills - coachability, business acumen, project management, and digital marketing - is crucial for a successful sales career. These skills not only enhance a sales professional's ability to meet and exceed targets but also equip them to navigate the complexities of modern sales environments effectively. By continually developing these skills, sales professionals can ensure they remain adaptable, informed, and successful in their careers.

5.8 Political Skills in Sales: Mastering the Art of Corporate Navigation

Getting ahead in the sales world requires more than just meeting quotas; it involves mastering the art of corporate navigation. Political skills, often misunderstood, are essential in understanding and influencing the workplace environment positively for your career growth. As I said earlier, being good at your job is only half the battle! The biggest tragedy is hard working, conscientious, dedicated salespeople, on whom the company depends for success and survival, not getting noticed and not getting promoted (and instead the wrong types getting noticed) because they neglected politics.

Understanding the Landscape of Workplace Politics

- **Assessing the Terrain:** Begin by immersing yourself in the company's culture. Pay close attention to both the formal structure and the less visible, but equally influential, informal networks. Understanding these dynamics is crucial as they often dictate the flow of information and decision-making processes within the organization. Observe the influencers, the decision-makers, and those who, while not in leadership positions, still wield significant influence.

- **Observational Skills:** Develop the ability to keenly observe and interpret office dynamics. This includes understanding non-verbal cues, recognizing patterns of interaction, and identifying allies and competitors. Being observant helps in navigating the workplace landscape without getting entangled in potential conflicts or missteps. It's about reading the room and understanding where and how you can contribute most effectively.

Cultivating Political Acumen

- **Building a Network of Allies:** Aim to establish a diverse network across various levels of the organization. This network should include not just those in leadership positions but also peers and junior colleagues who can offer different perspectives and support. The key is to build these relationships on a foundation of mutual respect and genuine interest, rather than merely for personal gain. Remember, a robust network is a rich source of insights, opportunities, and support.

- **Emotional Intelligence**: Emotional intelligence is crucial in managing and leveraging workplace relationships. It involves not only understanding your own emotions but also empathizing with others. This skill allows you to navigate complex social situations, communicate effectively, and build strong, trust-based relationships. It's about being aware of the emotional undercurrents in the workplace and responding to them in a way that fosters collaboration and respect.

Enhancing Visibility and Influence

- **Strategic Self-Promotion**: Learning how to strategically showcase your achievements is key. It's about finding the right moments and methods to highlight your contributions without overshadowing your colleagues. This could involve speaking up about your successes in team meetings or offering to lead projects that align with your skills and interests. The goal is to ensure that your efforts are recognized and associated with positive outcomes for the team and the company.

- **Positive Influence**: Strive to be a positive force within the organization. This means being proactive in meetings, offering constructive ideas, and being known as someone who contributes meaningfully. It's not just about being noticed; it's about being noticed for the right reasons – for being helpful, innovative, and a team player. Your aim should be to build a reputation as someone who adds value and positivity to the workplace.

Strategies for Career Growth

- **Mentorship and Sponsorship**: Seek out mentors who can provide guidance and sponsors who can advocate for you. A mentor helps you navigate your career path and grow professionally, while a sponsor can open doors to new opportunities and champion your cause in spaces where you may not have a voice. Both are invaluable in a corporate setting and can significantly influence your career trajectory.

- **Conflict Resolution**: Develop skills in diplomatically resolving conflicts. This involves being able to see different perspectives, mediate discussions, and find mutually beneficial solutions. Being seen as a problem-solver and a mediator enhances your reputation as a balanced and fair professional, which is invaluable in a corporate setting.

- **Personal Branding**: Cultivate a personal brand that aligns with your career aspirations and the organization's values. Consistently communicate this brand through your work ethic, professional achievements, and interactions with colleagues. Your personal brand should reflect your unique strengths and professional ethos, making you a memorable and respected member of the organization.

Political Complexities and Power Dynamics

- **Identifying Key Decision-Makers**: It's crucial to know who makes the decisions that could impact your career. Understand their criteria and align your strategies to be in sync with their decision-making processes. This requires a mix of strategic thinking and the ability to adapt your approach to different individuals' styles and preferences.

- **Influencing Without Authority**: Master the art of influencing others without direct authority. This includes using persuasion and negotiation skills, and the ability to present ideas in a compelling manner. It's about convincing others of the value of your ideas and contributions, thereby shaping decisions and outcomes even when you do not have formal authority.

- **Adapting to Change**: Be agile and adaptable to organizational changes. This could involve policy shifts, restructuring, or strategic directional changes. Adapting quickly and effectively to these changes not only shows your resilience but also positions you as a flexible and forward-thinking professional.

Building a Sustainable Network

- **Long-Term Relationship Building**: Focus on cultivating long-term relationships rather than seeking short-term gains. Genuine relationships built on trust and mutual respect are more sustainable and beneficial. They provide a support system within the organization, offering insights, advice, and assistance when needed.

- **Reciprocity**: Practice reciprocity in your professional relationships. Be ready to lend a hand or offer support in others' projects or initiatives. This approach fosters a culture of mutual support and collaboration, which is essential for a healthy work environment.

- **Consistent Engagement**: Keep regular contact with your professional network. This includes informal check-ins, sharing relevant and helpful information, and celebrating others' achievements. Staying engaged helps keep these relationships strong and active.

Mastering political skills in sales is about navigating the corporate environment strategically and ethically. It involves understanding the intricate web of relationships and power, building a network of allies, enhancing your visibility and influence, and adapting to organizational changes. These skills position you not just as a successful salesperson, but as a versatile professional capable of thriving in any corporate setting. The journey in mastering these skills is continuous, requiring keen observation, emotional intelligence, and strategic engagement. By honing these skills, you set the stage for a successful career.

5.8 Conclusion: Creating Your Own Path in Sales

As we encapsulate the journey of crafting a successful sales career, it's clear that a blend of specific ingredients and skills are fundamental. Emotional intelligence, self-awareness, and a robust sales acumen lay the groundwork for effective client interactions and decision-making. The significance of coachability, business acumen, project management, and digital marketing skills cannot be overstated in today's rapidly evolving sales landscape. These competencies enable you to navigate complex scenarios, understand and meet client needs, and stay ahead in a competitive field.

However, the essence of a rewarding sales career lies in personalizing your path. It involves recognizing your unique strengths and areas for growth, setting individual goals aligned with your aspirations, and continuously adapting and evolving. Every sales professional's journey is distinct, and embracing your individuality in this journey is key to long-term success and satisfaction.

In closing, remember that a career in sales is as challenging as it is rewarding. It offers a dynamic environment where resilience, adaptability, and continuous learning are not just required, but celebrated. As you forge your path in this exciting field, let your passion, curiosity, and commitment to excellence be your guide. Embrace each experience as an opportunity to grow, and you'll find that a career in sales can be not just successful, but deeply fulfilling.

Chapter 6: The Most Common Career Mistakes B2B Salespeople make ... and How to Avoid Them

6.1 Introduction to Common Career Mistakes

Embarking on a career in B2B sales can be both exhilarating and challenging. While the path to success is often marked by achievements and growth, it can also be littered with potential pitfalls. Recognizing and understanding these common career mistakes is crucial for any sales professional aiming to build a sustainable and rewarding career.

In the fast-paced and target-driven world of sales, professionals often encounter various traps. These can range from getting too comfortable in one's role, associating with the wrong crowd at work, to mismanaging one's personal brand. Other pitfalls include failing to strike a healthy work-life balance, which can lead to burnout, or not aligning one's career goals with personal values and skills. Such missteps, while seemingly insignificant at the outset, can have long-term impacts on career progression, job satisfaction, and personal well-being.

The key to avoiding these pitfalls lies in awareness and proactive management. Being conscious of these potential mistakes and understanding their implications allows sales professionals to navigate their careers more effectively. It involves regularly assessing one's career path, seeking feedback, and being open to change and self-improvement. This introductory chapter sets the stage for a deeper exploration of each of these pitfalls and offers guidance on how to avoid them, ensuring a thriving career in B2B sales.

6.2 The Pitfalls of Being 'One of the Boys/Girls'

In the collaborative world of sales, fostering good relationships with colleagues is important. However, there lies a subtle risk in becoming too closely aligned with certain groups, especially if they are known for underperformance or negativity. This phenomenon, often referred to as being 'one of the boys/girls,' can have unforeseen consequences on one's career trajectory.

Risks of Over-Associating with Underperformers or Complainers Aligning too closely with colleagues who are underperformers or habitual complainers can inadvertently affect your professional reputation. In sales, where results and attitudes are closely monitored, the company you keep can reflect on your own work ethic and professional outlook. There's a risk of guilt by association; if you're constantly seen with those who have a negative or lackadaisical approach to work, it might be assumed you share similar attitudes.

Moreover, such associations can impact your motivation and performance. Constant exposure to negativity or complacency can be demoralizing and may subconsciously lower your standards and expectations for your own performance.

Balancing Professional Relationships and Personal Friendships at Work Success in professional relationships and personal friendships in the workplace requires a delicate balance. It's important to be friendly and collaborative with all colleagues, but also crucial to maintain professional boundaries. This means being able to socialize and engage with your colleagues without being drawn into any negative dynamics they may harbor.

Developing emotional intelligence is key to managing these relationships effectively. Being empathetic and understanding towards your colleagues' situations can help in maintaining good relationships, while also remaining objective and focused on your own career goals.

Strategies for Maintaining a Positive, Professional Network Creating and maintaining a positive professional network involves strategic and intentional actions:

Diversify Your Network: Make an effort to connect with colleagues from different teams and hierarchical levels. This diversification not only broadens your professional network but also reduces the risk of being pigeonholed into one group.

Seek Positive Influences: Actively seek out and spend time with colleagues who are known for their positive attitude, strong performance, and professional success. Their drive and optimism can be infectious and inspiring.

Contribute Positively: Be known as someone who contributes positively to the workplace. This involves not just performing well in your role but also engaging in constructive conversations, offering help, and sharing knowledge.

Set Boundaries: Learn to set boundaries with colleagues who may have a negative influence on your professional image. This doesn't mean cutting off all interactions but rather being mindful of how deep these interactions go and how they might be perceived.

In conclusion, while being a part of the group is natural in a workplace, it's important to be mindful of the implications of these associations. By balancing professional relationships, actively building a positive network, and setting boundaries, you can maintain a healthy professional image and continue on a path to success in your sales career.

6.3 Reputation for Partying

In the world of sales, your professional image extends beyond your direct work performance; it encompasses your overall demeanour and conduct, including how you're perceived in social settings. A reputation for excessive partying can have a detrimental impact on how colleagues and clients view your professionalism.

Impact on Professional Image A party-centric reputation might initially seem harmless or even a way to be more relatable, especially in industries where socializing is part of the job. However, there's a fine line. When the line is crossed, it can lead to perceptions of irresponsibility or unreliability. Clients and colleagues might question your ability to handle sensitive information or critical tasks if they associate your image more with socializing than professionalism. This can lead to missed opportunities, as trust and reliability are cornerstones of successful business relationships.

Drawing Boundaries Between Personal and Professional Conduct Balancing your personal life with professional expectations is key. It's important to engage in company events and social gatherings as they can be valuable for team bonding and networking. However, maintaining a sense of decorum is crucial. This involves knowing your limits, being mindful of your behavior, and understanding how your actions might be perceived by others.

Tips for Professional Networking and Socializing

1. **Be Mindful of Social Media**: Remember that what you post on social media can blur the lines between personal and professional. Opt for a professional demeanour in platforms visible to colleagues and clients.

2. **Know Your Limits**: Be aware of your alcohol tolerance and how you conduct yourself under influence. It's often safer to err on the side of caution.

3. **Separate Social Circles**: While it's fine to have friends at work, it's wise to have distinct social circles for heavy partying and casual, professional networking.

4. **Lead with Professionalism**: At business events, focus on building genuine connections based on mutual professional interests rather than just socialising.

In essence, while socializing is an integral part of networking in sales, maintaining a balance is critical. A professional image that inspires confidence and trust will invariably be more beneficial to your career than a party-centric reputation.

6.4 Consequences of Excessive Drinking and Substance Use

In the high-pressure environment of sales, indulging in alcohol or substance use might appear as a common stress-reliever or a way to bond with clients and colleagues. However, excessive drinking and substance use can have serious repercussions, both on your professional life and personal health.

Impact on Career and Health Excessive drinking or substance use can severely impact your work performance. It can lead to decreased productivity, poor decision-making, and potentially even ethical lapses. Regular overindulgence may result in frequent absenteeism or showing up to work in an unfit state, which not only tarnishes your professional reputation but can also lead to job loss.

Healthwise, the impact can be equally severe. Long-term excessive drinking or substance use can lead to a host of health issues, including chronic diseases, mental health problems, and a general decline in physical and cognitive functions. This not only affects your ability to perform at work but also significantly diminishes your quality of life. It's also been the main cause of many, otherwise happy, relationship breakdowns.

Understanding the Importance of Moderation
Moderation is key in all aspects of life, including alcohol and substance use. It's important to set limits for yourself and stick to them. Being aware of the reasons why you might be inclined to overindulge can help in managing your consumption. Remember, there are healthier ways to deal with stress and pressure, such as exercise, hobbies, or seeking emotional support from friends, family, or professionals.

Seeking Support and Maintaining Professionalism
If you find yourself struggling with moderation, it's

important to seek help. Many organisations offer support programs for employees, and there are numerous external resources available for those needing assistance. Addressing the issue proactively is a sign of strength, not weakness.

Maintaining professionalism means recognizing the impact of your actions on your career and health and taking steps to ensure you remain effective and reliable in your professional role. In the competitive world of sales, your health and reputation are invaluable assets that should be protected and nurtured. Your personal and romantic relationships are just as important (if not more so) than your career success. Or, to put it another way, you'll be more successful at work if you have your personal life in good shape.

In summary, while the occasional social drink is a norm in many professional settings, it is crucial to be mindful of the long-term consequences of excessive drinking and substance use. Moderation, self-awareness, and seeking support when necessary are vital to maintaining both your health and your professional standing.

6.5 Managing Your Reputation and Personal Brand

In the world of sales, reputation and personal branding are not just ancillary aspects of your career; they are central to it. Your reputation often precedes you in meetings, negotiations, and even before you enter a room. It's the aggregation of every interaction, every deal, and every relationship you've built, while your personal brand is how you consciously shape and project these elements to the world.

Significance of Reputation and Personal Brand in Sales A strong reputation and personal brand can open doors to new opportunities, help build more meaningful relationships with clients, and set you apart in a competitive field. In sales, where trust and credibility are paramount, a solid reputation can be your greatest asset. It can lead to referrals, repeat business, and a network that actively supports and promotes you.

Your personal brand, on the other hand, is how you differentiate yourself from other sales professionals. It's what you stand for, your unique selling proposition, and how you communicate your value to clients and colleagues. It's about being memorable for the right reasons.

Techniques for Building and Maintaining a Positive Professional Image

1. **Consistent Professionalism**: Ensure that all your interactions reflect professionalism. This includes everything from punctuality and the way you dress to how you handle difficult situations and communicate in emails.

2. **Deliver on Promises**: Your reputation is built on reliability. Always strive to meet your commitments, and if you can't, communicate proactively. Under promise and over deliver as often as possible.

3. **Engage in Continuous Learning**: Stay informed about your industry and refine your sales skills. This will not only improve your performance but also demonstrate your commitment to excellence.

4. **Contribute to Your Community**: Share your knowledge, be it through mentoring, writing articles, or speaking at industry events. This positions you as a thought leader and enhances your professional image.

5. **Act Like a Professional**: Don't lie or cheat on your expenses, and get them submitted on time! Treat your 'paperwork' (forecasts, pipeline reports, quarterly business plans, etc) seriously – not as something you'll rush 5

minutes before it's due. Things like that make a real difference to how your perceived.

6. **Dress & Present Yourself for Success**: You've heard it before: "dress for 2 roles above yours". Don't be a lazy slob with your grooming and appearance. Dress conservatively. If you really want to get your face tattooed, fine go ahead. Just accept that it will affect how the world perceives you.

Regularly Auditing Your Online and Offline Presence In the digital age, your online presence is a critical component of your personal brand. Regular audits of your social media profiles, personal website, and any content you publish online are essential. Ensure that what you post aligns with the professional image you want to project. This includes not just your posts but also your comments, shares, and the groups or pages you associate with.

Offline, be mindful of how you present yourself in networking events, conferences, and even casual meetings. Every interaction is a chance to reinforce your brand. Regularly ask for feedback from peers, mentors, or clients to understand how you are perceived and where you can improve.

In conclusion, managing your reputation and personal brand in sales is about consciously shaping how you are perceived in both online and offline interactions. It's a continuous process of aligning your actions, communications, and learning with the professional image you want to project. By carefully curating your reputation and brand, you can significantly impact your career trajectory and success in the sales world.

6.6 Course Correction in Career Decisions

In the dynamic landscape of a sales career, not every decision regarding job roles or industry alignment turns out as expected. Recognizing when you've made a poor choice and having the adaptability to course-correct is crucial for long-term success and satisfaction in your career.

Recognizing Poor Job or Industry Choices The first step in course correction is acknowledging that a job or industry may not be the right fit. This realization often stems from consistent feelings of dissatisfaction, lack of motivation, or a realization that your skills and values do not align with your current role or industry. It might also manifest as a sense of stagnation, where personal and professional growth seems halted.

Poor fits can result from various factors: a company culture that doesn't align with your values, a role that doesn't utilise your strengths, or an industry that doesn't excite you. It's important to identify the root cause to understand whether the issue is with the specific job role, the company, or the industry as a whole.

Adaptability and Openness to Change Adaptability is key in effectively managing your career. It involves being open to exploring new roles, industries, or even retraining if necessary. The willingness to learn and pivot is essential, especially in a field as dynamic as sales, where industry trends and required skills can change rapidly.

Being adaptable also means being proactive about seeking new opportunities, whether within your current organisation or outside it. Regularly updating your resume, networking, and staying informed about industry trends are all part of this adaptive approach.

Strategies for Career Shifts

1. **Self-Assessment**: Regularly evaluate your job satisfaction, professional goals, and personal values. This helps in understanding whether your current role aligns with your career aspirations.

2. **Seek Feedback**: Talk to mentors, colleagues, or industry contacts. They can provide an

outside perspective and may offer insights you hadn't considered.

3. **Research and Plan**: If considering a shift, research new roles or industries thoroughly. Understand the skills required and how they match with your current skill set. Plan for any additional training or education you might need.

4. **Take Calculated Risks**: Don't be afraid to step out of your comfort zone, but do so with calculated risks. This might involve taking on a new project, a different role, or even changing industries.

In summary, course correction in your sales career is about recognizing misalignments, being adaptable to change, and strategically planning your next steps. It's about making informed decisions that steer your career in a direction that aligns with your personal and professional goals.

6.7 Financial Patience and Planning

A career in sales often comes with the promise of lucrative financial rewards. However, navigating the waters of financial aspirations requires a balanced approach, combining patience with prudent planning. Understanding the timing and trajectory of financial success in sales is critical to avoid the pitfalls of unrealistic expectations and ensure long-term satisfaction and stability.

Balancing Financial Aspirations The journey to financial success in sales is rarely linear. Early in your career, you might face a period where income does not immediately meet expectations. It's crucial during these times to maintain financial patience. Rushing towards high-income opportunities without the necessary experience or jumping into high-stakes deals without adequate preparation can lead to setbacks. Conversely, delaying success due to fear of taking risks or complacency can hinder your financial growth. Striking a balance involves recognizing your current skill level, continuously striving for improvement, and seizing appropriate opportunities that come your way.

Long-term Financial Planning and Career Choices Financial success in sales is best approached with a long-term perspective. This involves setting realistic financial goals and aligning them with your career path. Consider the typical earnings trajectory in your specific field of sales, and plan your career moves accordingly. This might involve strategic job changes, additional training, or expanding your sales portfolio.

Effective financial planning also means managing your earnings wisely. This includes budgeting, saving, investing, and even seeking professional financial advice. Building a financial cushion can provide the security to take calculated risks in your career, like transitioning to a role with a higher potential income but a longer ramp-up time.

Avoiding Unrealistic Financial Expectations
Unrealistic financial expectations can lead to frustration and impulsive career decisions. Avoid setting your financial goals based solely on the highest earners in your field, as their success might involve variables not immediately applicable to your situation.

Stay informed about the industry standards for compensation in your field and region. This knowledge helps in setting achievable financial targets and negotiating salaries or commissions. Also, recognize that financial success in sales often comes with experience, skills development, and building a strong client base.

In conclusion, financial patience and planning are key to achieving sustainable success in a sales career. It involves balancing aspirations with realistic goals, making informed career choices, and wise financial management.

6.8 Staying Too Long vs. Leaving Too Soon

A fruitful career in sales involves making pivotal decisions about when to stay in a role and when to move on. The timing of these decisions can significantly impact your professional growth and job satisfaction. Understanding when to embrace a new challenge or when to consolidate your position is crucial for a balanced and successful career trajectory.

Recognizing When It's Time to Move On Knowing when to leave a role or company is often a mix of intuition and objective assessment. Key indicators that it might be time to move on include a lack of learning opportunities, no room for advancement, or a misalignment with your long-term career goals. If you find yourself no longer feeling challenged, or if the role stops contributing to your skill development and professional growth, these are signs it might be time to seek new opportunities.

Another factor is the work environment. If the company culture or values are in conflict with your own, or if there is a persistent negative impact on your well-being, these are strong indicators that a change is needed.

The Risks of Staying in Your Comfort Zone
Comfort zones are safe but they are often barriers to growth. Staying too long in a role that no longer challenges you can lead to stagnation. It can diminish your marketability as you miss out on learning new skills or technologies that are evolving in the industry.

Staying put due to fear of change or failure can also limit your career potential. Taking risks and embracing new challenges is essential for growth. It exposes you to new experiences, broadens your skill set, and can lead to more fulfilling work.

Assessing Career Moves and Readiness for New Challenges When contemplating a career move, start with a self-assessment. Evaluate your current skills, achievements, and how they align with your career aspirations. Consider what you seek in a new role — whether it's more responsibility, a different company culture, or a new industry.

Research potential roles and companies thoroughly. Understand the skills and experiences required and assess how they match with your current profile. Consider the potential for growth and learning in the new role.

Networking can also provide insights into potential opportunities and the realities of different roles. Reach out to contacts in your desired field or company to gather firsthand information about the work environment and expectations.

Finally, plan your transition strategically. This might involve upskilling for the new role, updating your resume, or even seeking mentorship to prepare for the change.

In summary, the decision to stay in a role or move on should be based on a careful evaluation of your current situation and future aspirations. Balancing the comfort of familiar roles with the excitement and growth potential of new challenges is key to a dynamic and rewarding career in sales. It's about making informed decisions that align with your long-term professional goals and personal growth.

6.9 The Importance of Setting Goals

In the fast-paced world of sales, setting clear and achievable career goals is not just beneficial; it's essential. Goals provide direction, motivate you to push through challenges, and serve as benchmarks for measuring success. They are the roadmap guiding your career journey, helping to ensure that each step you take is purposeful and aligned with your broader aspirations.

Setting Clear, Achievable Career Goals The process of setting goals in sales should be strategic and thoughtful. Begin by defining what success looks like for you. This might involve specific sales targets, acquiring new skills, or progressing to a higher role. Ensure that your goals are Specific, Measurable, Achievable, Relevant, and Time-bound (SMART). For instance, rather than a vague goal like "increase sales," aim for something more tangible, like "increase sales by 20% within the next six months."

It's also important to balance ambition with realism. While it's good to push yourself, setting overly ambitious goals that are out of reach can lead to frustration and demotivation. Your goals should stretch your abilities but remain attainable with hard work and dedication.

Regularly Reviewing and Adjusting Goals The world of sales is dynamic, with frequent changes in market conditions, client needs, and product offerings. This fluidity necessitates regular reviews and adjustments of your goals. Assess your progress periodically and be ready to recalibrate your goals in response to new challenges and opportunities. This might mean shifting your focus, developing new strategies, or even pursuing additional training or mentorship.

Aligning Goals with Personal Values and Career Aspirations Ultimately, the most fulfilling and sustainable goals are those that align with your personal values and long-term career aspirations. Reflect on what matters most to you in your career – whether it's making meaningful connections, contributing to a team, personal growth, or financial success. Ensure that your goals reflect these values, as this alignment will provide deeper motivation and satisfaction.

In conclusion, setting clear, achievable, and meaningful goals is a fundamental practice for anyone in the sales profession. It's about knowing where you want to go and planning the steps to get there. By regularly reviewing and adjusting your goals in line with market dynamics and your personal values, you can navigate your sales career with confidence and purpose. This goal-setting approach not only fosters professional growth but also ensures a sense of accomplishment in your sales journey.

6.10 The Importance of Managing Your Manager as a Novice Sales Professional

For a novice in the sales profession, mastering the early stages of your career is as much about selling products or services as it is about managing relationships, particularly the one with your manager. This relationship is pivotal; your manager not only plays a key role in your current job satisfaction and performance but also significantly influences your career progression.

Gaining Promotion and Avoiding Veto One of the most critical aspects of managing your manager is understanding that they largely hold the key to your promotions. Their endorsement is often essential for moving up the career ladder. Managers not only assess your performance but also advocate for your capabilities to higher-ups. Therefore, ensuring that your manager recognizes and appreciates your contributions is crucial. This doesn't mean relentless self-promotion but rather consistently delivering on your targets and responsibilities, actively seeking feedback, and demonstrating your commitment to personal and professional growth.

Leveraging Their Power and Credibility Managers typically have more power and credibility within the organization due to their experience and position. By effectively managing your relationship with them, you can leverage this to your advantage. Learn from their experiences and insights. Managers can provide valuable mentorship, help you navigate company politics, and guide you in complex sales scenarios. Building a strong rapport based on respect and trust can make your manager more inclined to invest in your development and advocate on your behalf.

Aligning Skills with Company Goals For career advancement, especially in sales, it's crucial that your skills and contributions align with the company's objectives. Managers play a critical role in this alignment. They can provide clarity on company goals, performance expectations, and how your role contributes to the broader objectives. Understanding and aligning with these goals will not only enhance your performance but also position you as a valuable asset to the team.

Effective Communication and Feedback

Open and effective communication with your manager is key. Regular check-ins and updates about your progress and challenges help keep your manager informed and engaged in your development. Seek constructive feedback and be open to suggestions and guidance. Demonstrating that you value and act on their feedback can strengthen your relationship and show your dedication to improving.

Proactive Problem-Solving and Initiative

Managers appreciate team members who are proactive and can solve problems independently. Taking initiative in addressing challenges, seeking solutions, and being resourceful reflects positively on your capabilities. It also reduces the burden on your manager, showcasing your potential for greater responsibilities.

In conclusion, effectively managing your relationship with your manager is a critical skill for a novice sales professional. It involves understanding the nuances of this dynamic and treating it with respect, proactive communication, and alignment with company goals. Building a positive relationship with your manager can lead to mentorship opportunities, better performance assessment, and support in your career progression. It's about demonstrating your value, learning from their experience, and ensuring that your growth trajectory aligns with the company's vision. Remember, in sales, your ability to manage relationships doesn't just apply to clients but is equally important within your own organization, starting with your manager. By successfully managing this relationship, you lay the groundwork for a fruitful and advancing career in sales.

6.11 Conclusion: Avoiding Career Pitfalls

In the journey of a sales career, being aware of and skilfully tip toing around common pitfalls is as important as capitalizing on the right opportunities. The key to avoiding these career mistakes lies in a blend of self-awareness, proactive career management, and continuous learning.

The first step to avoiding career pitfalls is recognizing them. Whether it's getting too comfortable in a role, aligning with underperforming colleagues, or failing to maintain a professional image, awareness is crucial. Cultivating a balanced approach to professional relationships, managing your personal brand diligently, and being mindful of your conduct in and out of the workplace are essential strategies.

Proactive career management involves setting clear goals, regularly assessing your career trajectory, and being open to change and adaptation. It's about making informed decisions, whether it's time to switch roles or industries, and not being afraid to step out of your comfort zone for better opportunities.

Take charge of your career by continuously seeking opportunities for growth and development. This could mean pursuing further education, seeking mentorship, or simply taking on new challenges within your current role. Regularly update your skills and knowledge to stay relevant in the ever-evolving field of sales.

Remember, each mistake is an opportunity to learn and grow. Embracing your missteps as valuable learning experiences can transform them into stepping stones towards success. Your career in sales is a journey of constant evolution – one where resilience, adaptability, and continual learning pave the way to success and fulfillment. Stay motivated, stay curious, and let each experience, good or bad, enrich your professional journey in sales.

Chapter 7: Potential Career Paths After 3 Years in Sales

In the dynamic world of sales, numerous career paths unfold as you gain experience. After approximately three to five years, a sales professional is often at a crossroads, equipped with skills and knowledge ready to be applied in various directions. This chapter explores common career paths, along with a few additional options, offering insights into each and guiding you on what to expect and how to transition successfully.

This comprehensive chapter outline is designed to help sales professionals, especially those with around three years of experience, understand the various career paths available to them. It highlights the skills needed for each path, the challenges one might face, and strategies for a successful transition. By considering personal strengths, interests, and market demands, sales professionals can make informed decisions about their career progression and growth.

7.1 Advancing to a Senior Sales Role

After three years in the sales industry, advancing to a senior sales role is a natural progression for many professionals. This move not only signifies a step up in responsibilities and potential earnings but also marks a transition in your career where your skills, experience, and knowledge are recognized and expanded upon.

Transitioning to Senior Sales

- Preparation: Begin by assessing your current skill set and identifying areas for improvement. Reflect on your sales achievements, client feedback, and any recurring challenges you've faced.

- Skills Audit: Compare your skills with the requirements of a senior sales role. This might include enhanced negotiation skills, strategic planning, and advanced product knowledge.

- Training and Development: Consider additional training or certifications that could bolster your qualifications for a senior role. This could involve advanced sales courses, leadership training, or industry-specific seminars.

Skills Enhancement

- Strategic Selling: Senior sales roles often require a more strategic approach to selling. This involves understanding larger market trends, developing long-term sales plans, and tailoring strategies to diverse client segments.

- Leadership: While you may not be managing a team directly, leadership skills are crucial. You'll need to lead client meetings, mentor junior sales staff, and potentially lead project teams.

- Client Management: Managing key accounts or high-value clients is often part of senior sales roles. This requires an ability to build deep, long-term relationships and understand complex client needs.

Networking and Visibility

- Internal Networking: Increase your visibility within the company. Engage with different departments, understand their roles in the sales process, and how you can collaborate effectively.

- Building a Reputation: Consistently demonstrate your sales expertise and contributions. Share your successes and learnings with your team and superiors.

- Seeking a Mentor: Find a mentor who is experienced in senior sales roles. They can provide invaluable advice, introduce you to new opportunities, and help you navigate your career path.

Conclusion

Advancing to a senior sales role is a significant career milestone that requires preparation, skill enhancement, and strategic networking. It's an opportunity to leverage your experience, take on greater responsibilities, and further your sales career. Focus on developing a strategic approach to sales, enhancing your leadership capabilities, and building a strong professional network. With these strategies in place, you'll be well-positioned to step into a senior sales role and succeed.

7.2 Becoming an SDR/Inside Sales Manager

Transitioning from a sales role to managing a team as an SDR (Sales Development Representative) or Inside Sales Manager is a significant step that involves a shift from individual performance to leading a team towards collective success. This role requires not only a deep understanding of sales processes but also strong leadership and people management skills.

Role and Responsibilities

- Understanding the Managerial Role: As an SDR/Inside Sales Manager, your primary role shifts from selling to managing the sales process and leading a team. This includes setting team targets, monitoring progress, and ensuring your team is motivated and equipped to meet their goals.

- Team Management: You are responsible for hiring, training, and developing your team. This involves identifying skill gaps, providing ongoing coaching, and addressing performance issues.

- Strategic Planning: Developing and implementing sales strategies that align with the company's goals. This includes optimizing sales processes and workflows.

Leadership Skills

- Developing Leadership Qualities: Effective leadership involves inspiring and motivating your team. Work on skills like empathy, communication, and the ability to provide clear and constructive feedback.

- Conflict Resolution: Be prepared to handle conflicts within your team, whether they are performance-related or interpersonal.

- Leading by Example: Maintain a high standard of professionalism and work ethic. Your team will look to you as a role model in terms of behavior and sales tactics.

Performance Management

- Setting Clear Expectations: Clearly define what is expected from each team member in terms of targets and behaviors.

- Monitoring and Reporting: Regularly review team performance against targets. Use data and metrics to make informed decisions about strategy and training needs.

- Motivation and Incentives: Understand what motivates your team members and develop incentive programs to keep them engaged and driven.

Conclusion

Becoming an SDR/Inside Sales Manager is a challenging yet rewarding transition. It requires a combination of sales expertise, strategic planning, and strong leadership abilities. By focusing on effective team management, developing your leadership skills, and implementing robust performance management strategies, you can successfully guide your team to achieve their targets and contribute significantly to the company's sales objectives.

This role is not just about managing; it's about inspiring and cultivating a successful sales environment. Your ability to lead, motivate, and develop your team will be key to your success in this role. Remember, the transition to a managerial position is also a learning journey – one that will enhance your professional growth and provide valuable experiences for future career advancements. Embrace this opportunity to shape the careers of your team members while also carving out a significant leadership role for yourself within the organization.

7.3 Moving into Sales Operations

Transitioning into Sales Operations after gaining experience in direct sales roles offers a unique opportunity to influence the sales process from a strategic and analytical standpoint. Sales Operations focuses on the efficiency and effectiveness of a sales team, requiring a distinct set of skills and a deep understanding of sales mechanics.

Understanding Sales Operations

- Role Scope: Sales Operations involves managing the essential behind-the-scenes activities that support the sales team. This includes sales strategy planning, managing tools and technology, overseeing sales data and analytics, and streamlining the sales process.

- Impact on Sales Efficiency: Your role is pivotal in ensuring the sales team operates efficiently. This includes everything from optimizing lead management to refining sales methodologies and ensuring the CRM system is utilized effectively.

Analytical Skills

- Data-Driven Decision Making: In Sales Operations, decisions are often backed by data. Developing skills in data analysis, interpreting sales metrics, and converting insights into actionable strategies is crucial.

- Sales Forecasting: You will be responsible for forecasting sales trends, which requires an ability to analyze past sales data and market conditions, and predict future sales performance.

Cross-Functional Collaboration

- Working with Different Departments: Sales Operations often involves collaboration with marketing, finance, and customer service teams to ensure cohesive sales strategies and operations.

- Process Optimization: Identify areas where sales processes can be streamlined or improved. This might involve implementing new sales tools, refining lead qualification processes, or improving communication channels between departments.

Skills Development for Sales Operations

- Learning New Technologies: Stay updated with the latest sales tools and technologies. Understanding how these tools can enhance sales processes is key.

- Project Management: Strong organizational and project management skills are essential. You'll often oversee multiple projects aimed at improving sales efficiency.

Conclusion

Moving into Sales Operations is a significant shift from being directly involved in sales. It requires a strategic mindset, a keen eye for data and analytics, and the ability to manage cross-functional projects. This role allows you to play a critical part in shaping the sales strategy and infrastructure of your organization. You will be instrumental in driving the sales team towards higher performance through efficient processes and systems.

Embracing this role means moving beyond individual sales targets to a broader view of the sales organization's success. It's about understanding the bigger picture and using your sales experience to enhance the overall sales framework. As a Sales Operations professional, your work directly contributes to the foundational strength of the sales team, making your role both challenging and impactful.

In summary, transitioning into Sales Operations opens up a new avenue in your sales career where your analytical skills, strategic planning, and cross-functional collaboration come to the forefront. It's an opportunity to leverage your sales experience in a different dimension, ensuring the smooth operation and success of the sales engine of the company.

7.4 Transitioning to Content Marketing

After a few years in sales, transitioning to content marketing can be a rewarding career move. This path leverages your deep understanding of customer needs and sales processes, enabling you to create compelling marketing content that resonates with your audience and drives sales.

Leveraging Sales Experience in Content Marketing

- Understanding Customer Pain Points: Use your sales experience to identify common challenges and questions your customers have. This insight is invaluable in creating content that addresses these pain points effectively.

- Sales Insights for Content Creation: Reflect on your sales interactions to generate ideas for content that can help guide customers through the buying process.

Content Strategy and Development

- Developing a Content Strategy: Learn to develop a content strategy that aligns with the company's sales goals and marketing objectives. This includes identifying the right channels, formats, and messages to reach and engage your target audience.

- Creating Engaging Content: Use storytelling and your sales experiences to create engaging and informative content. This might include blog posts, case studies, videos, and infographics that educate and persuade potential customers.

Digital Marketing Knowledge

- Understanding Digital Platforms: Familiarize yourself with various digital marketing platforms and how they can be used to distribute and amplify content.

- SEO and Analytics: Gain a basic understanding of Search Engine Optimization (SEO) and how to use analytics to measure the effectiveness of your content. Learn to interpret data to refine your content strategy and improve engagement.

Transition Skills

- Writing and Communication Skills: Strong writing and communication skills are essential. Consider taking courses or workshops to hone your writing ability for different formats and audiences.

- Collaboration with Sales and Marketing Teams: Work closely with sales and marketing teams to ensure content aligns with sales objectives and marketing campaigns. Your sales background provides a unique perspective that can bridge the gap between these two functions.

Conclusion

Transitioning from sales to content marketing opens up a creative avenue where you can directly influence the buyer's journey. It allows you to use your understanding of the customer's mind and the sales process in a new and impactful way. In content marketing, your goal shifts from direct selling to creating narratives and materials that attract, inform, and engage potential customers, nurturing them towards a sale.

This career path is not just about writing and creativity; it's about strategically using content to drive sales and business growth. With the right approach, transitioning to content marketing can be a seamless and rewarding next step in your sales career, allowing you to play a crucial role in the broader sales and marketing strategy of your organization.

7.5 Becoming a Customer Success Manager

After honing skills in sales, transitioning to a Customer Success Manager role can be a very rewarding and beneficial career path. This role focuses on nurturing and maintaining relationships with existing customers, ensuring their continued satisfaction and loyalty, and ultimately contributing to the company's sustained success.

Focus on Customer Retention

- Shifting from Acquisition to Retention: Unlike the primary focus of acquiring new customers in sales, as a Customer Success Manager, your goal is to retain and grow existing customer accounts. This involves understanding their ongoing needs and ensuring they achieve their desired outcomes with your product or service.

- Long-Term Relationship Building: Develop strategies to maintain and strengthen long-term relationships with customers, focusing on their continuous success and satisfaction.

Building Long-Term Relationships

- Understanding Customer Needs: Utilize your sales experience to deeply understand customer requirements and expectations. This knowledge is crucial in tailoring your approach to each customer's unique situation.

- Proactive Communication: Regularly communicate with customers to check on their progress, offer help, and gather feedback. This proactive approach helps in identifying and addressing any issues early on.

Product Expertise and Consultation

- Becoming a Product Expert: Gain comprehensive knowledge of your company's products or services to provide expert advice and solutions to customers. Your insight will help customers maximize the value they get from your offerings.

- Problem-Solving and Consultation: Apply your problem-solving skills from sales to help customers overcome challenges. Offer consultation and guidance to assist them in achieving their objectives with your product.

Skills Development for Customer Success

- Developing Soft Skills: Enhance your communication, empathy, and problem-solving skills. These are key in building rapport and effectively addressing customer needs.

- Analytical Skills: Develop the ability to analyze customer usage data to gain insights into customer health and predict potential churn. Use this data to implement strategies for customer retention and satisfaction.

Conclusion

Transitioning to a Customer Success Manager is a significant shift from the direct pursuit of sales targets. It offers an opportunity to contribute to the company's growth by ensuring customers are successful and satisfied with their investment. This role requires a blend of relationship management, product expertise, and a consultative approach, all of which are crucial in fostering customer loyalty and long-term business success.

In this role, your impact goes beyond individual sales achievements. You play a vital role in customer retention and advocacy, directly influencing the company's reputation and recurring revenue. It's a path that allows for deepening customer relationships and ensuring the long-term success of both the customers and the company.

Embracing this role means shifting your focus to a more holistic view of the customer journey, where your efforts are directed towards nurturing lasting customer engagement and satisfaction. With the right approach and commitment to continuous learning and adaptation, a career as a Customer Success Manager can be highly rewarding, offering diverse challenges and the satisfaction of directly impacting customer experiences and outcomes.

7.6 Pre-Sales Consultant / Engineer

Transitioning to a Pre-Sales Consultant or Engineer role after gaining experience in sales is a strategic career move for those interested in combining technical expertise with customer interaction. This role is crucial in the sales process, focusing on the technical aspects of sales proposals and product demonstrations.

Technical Proficiency

- Developing Technical Skills: As a Pre-Sales Consultant or Engineer, a deep understanding of the product's technical aspects is essential. This might require additional training or certification, especially if you are moving from a purely sales-focused role.

- Product Demonstration Skills: Learn how to effectively demonstrate the product, highlighting its features and benefits in a way that addresses the specific needs and pain points of each client.

Consultative Selling

- Solution-Based Approach: The role involves a consultative approach to selling, where you work closely with potential clients to understand their requirements and provide solutions that meet these needs.

- Customizing Proposals: Tailor proposals to suit the unique challenges and objectives of each client. This involves not just technical customization but also a clear understanding of how the product fits into the client's broader business context.

Working with Sales Teams

- Collaboration: Work closely with the sales team to ensure that the technical aspects of the product are accurately represented and align with the overall sales strategy.

- Technical Support for Sales: Act as the technical expert during sales meetings and calls, providing the necessary technical backing for the sales arguments and helping the sales team overcome any technical objections raised by prospects.

Skills Development for Pre-Sales

- Technical Communication: Enhance your ability to communicate complex technical information in a clear, concise, and understandable manner for non-technical clients.

- Problem-Solving: Hone your problem-solving skills to address technical challenges and queries raised by potential clients during the sales process.

Conclusion

Transitioning into a Pre-Sales Consultant or Engineer role offers an opportunity to delve deeper into the technical side of sales. It is a role that bridges the gap between technical expertise and customer interaction, playing a critical part in the sales cycle. This position requires not only technical knowledge but also the ability to present this knowledge in a client-friendly manner.

In this role, your contribution goes beyond just selling a product; you become an integral part of the client's decision-making process, helping them understand how the product can solve their specific problems and meet their needs. The role is ideal for those who enjoy the technical aspects of products and services and are adept at communicating these details effectively to help close sales deals.

7.7 Product Management

For sales professionals with a few years of experience, transitioning into product management presents an exciting opportunity to leverage their customer and market knowledge to drive product strategy and development. Product managers play a critical role in guiding the success of a product from conception to launch and beyond.

Transition to Product Management

- Utilising Sales Experience: Use your understanding of customer needs, feedback, and market trends gained from your sales experience to inform product development and positioning.

- Bridging Sales and Development: As a product manager, you become the link between the sales team, customers, and the product development team, ensuring that customer insights are translated into product features.

Cross-Functional Leadership

- Collaborating with Teams: Work with various teams, including engineering, design, marketing, and sales, to develop and execute a cohesive product strategy.

- Communication and Coordination: Develop strong communication and coordination skills to manage diverse team inputs and align everyone towards common product goals.

Market Analysis and Product Strategy

- Conducting Market Research: Regularly conduct and analyze market research to understand industry trends, competitor products, and evolving customer needs.

- Strategic Planning: Create and implement a strategic plan for the product, including defining the product vision, setting goals, and prioritizing features based on market and customer requirements.

Skills Development for Product Management

- Product Lifecycle Knowledge: Gain a deep understanding of the product lifecycle, from ideation and development to launch and iteration.

- Analytical Skills: Enhance your ability to analyze market data and customer feedback to make informed product decisions.

- Project Management: Develop project management skills to oversee the product development process, ensuring that timelines, budgets, and product quality standards are met.

Conclusion

Moving into product management allows you to apply your sales acumen in a new domain, directly influencing the creation and improvement of products. This role requires a combination of market insight, strategic thinking, and cross-functional leadership.

In this role, you have the opportunity to shape the future of a product, making decisions that not only impact its success in the market but also the overall success of the company. It's a role that demands a broad perspective, understanding not just what customers want now, but anticipating future trends and needs.

Your sales background gives you a unique edge in product management. You bring firsthand customer insights, an understanding of the competitive landscape, and a keen sense of what makes a product sell. This transition can be deeply rewarding, offering a chance to see the tangible results of your strategies and decisions in the product's market performance.

Embracing a career in product management means stepping into a role where your decisions have a direct impact on the product's journey and its users. It's a path that combines creativity with strategy, customer insight with innovation, offering a dynamic and influential career trajectory for sales professionals looking to expand their horizons.

7.8 Sales Training and Development

Transitioning into sales training and development is a natural progression for sales professionals who have a passion for mentoring and coaching others. This role involves educating new sales hires, developing sales training programs, and fostering a culture of continuous improvement within the sales team.

Educator Role

- Shifting from Selling to Teaching: Embrace the change from being a salesperson to becoming an educator. This involves using your sales experience to teach others about effective sales techniques and strategies.

- Curriculum Development: Develop a comprehensive training curriculum that covers all aspects of the sales process, from prospecting and qualifying leads to closing deals and managing customer relationships.

Curriculum Development

- Sales Process and Methodologies: Include training modules on different sales processes and methodologies, tailoring them to fit the company's approach and industry specifics.

- Role-Playing and Practical Exercises: Incorporate practical exercises, such as role-playing scenarios, to help trainees apply theoretical knowledge in real-life sales situations.

Mentoring and Coaching

- One-on-One Coaching: Provide personalized coaching to new sales hires, helping them to overcome specific challenges and improve their sales skills.

- Ongoing Development: Establish a system for ongoing training and development, ensuring that the sales team stays updated on the latest sales trends and techniques.

Skills Development for Sales Training

- Communication Skills: As a sales trainer, your ability to clearly and effectively communicate information is crucial. Focus on honing these skills to ensure your training is impactful.

- Feedback and Evaluation: Learn to provide constructive feedback and evaluate the performance of sales trainees effectively. This will help them grow and improve continuously.

Conclusion

Moving into sales training and development is an enriching career path that allows you to share your knowledge and experience with others. It's a role that not only impacts the professional growth of individual team members but also contributes to the overall success of the sales organization.

In this role, you have the opportunity to shape the sales culture and create a legacy of well-trained, skilled sales professionals. It's a path that requires patience, excellent communication skills, and a deep understanding of the sales process. By embracing this role, you can make a lasting impact on the careers of many and contribute significantly to the growth and success of your organization.

7.9 Business Development & Go-To-Market

For sales professionals looking to expand their horizon beyond direct sales, a career in Business Development offers a blend of strategic planning, relationship building, and market expansion. This role is crucial for identifying new business opportunities, forging strategic partnerships, and driving the growth of the company.

Strategic Partnerships

- Identifying Potential Partnerships: Use your sales acumen to identify potential strategic partners that align with the company's goals and objectives. This involves understanding both your company's and the potential partner's strengths, weaknesses, and market positions.

- Negotiating Partnerships: Develop negotiation skills to structure mutually beneficial partnerships. This includes contract negotiation, setting partnership terms, and aligning partnership goals with company strategies.

Market Expansion Strategies

- Analyzing Market Opportunities: Conduct market research to identify new market opportunities. This could include new geographical regions or different customer segments.

- Developing Market Entry Plans: Create strategic plans for entering new markets. This involves understanding the market dynamics, customer needs, and potential barriers to entry.

Relationship Building with Key Stakeholders

- Networking and Relationship Management: Leverage and expand your professional network to include industry influencers and decision-makers. Effective relationship management is key to opening doors to new opportunities.

- Building Credibility: Position yourself and your company as credible and reliable partners. This involves not just talking about your company's products or services but also demonstrating a deep understanding of the potential partner's challenges and needs.

Skills Development for Business Development

- Strategic Thinking: Develop a strategic mindset, focusing on long-term goals and the bigger picture of business growth.

- Communication Skills: Enhance your ability to communicate effectively, especially when it comes to presenting ideas and persuading stakeholders.

- Project Management: Develop project management skills, as business development often involves overseeing projects from the initial idea to execution.

Conclusion

Transitioning into a Business Development role allows you to use your sales skills in a broader context. It's not just about selling a product or service but about finding new ways to grow the business. This could be through new market opportunities, strategic partnerships, or innovative business models.

In this role, your impact goes beyond meeting sales targets; you contribute directly to the strategic growth of the company. It's a challenging yet rewarding career path that requires a mix of strategic thinking, relationship building, and a deep understanding of market dynamics. Embracing this role means becoming a key player in shaping the future direction of the company.

7.10 Entrepreneurial Ventures

For sales professionals with a strong desire to forge their own path, venturing into entrepreneurship is a thrilling and challenging career choice. After years in sales, leveraging your experience, network, and skills to start your own business can be a natural progression.

Starting Your Own Business

- Utilising Sales Experience: Apply your sales experience to understand customer needs and market demands. This is crucial in identifying business opportunities and developing products or services that meet those needs.

- Business Planning: Develop a comprehensive business plan that outlines your business idea, target market, competition, business model, and financial projections. This plan will be your roadmap and is also essential if you seek funding.

Business Planning and Fundraising

- Understanding Financing Options: Learn about different funding options, such as bootstrapping, venture capital, angel investors, or bank loans. Understand the pros and cons of each to make informed decisions about funding your venture.

- Pitching to Investors: Develop your pitching skills. A compelling pitch is crucial to securing funding from investors. It should clearly articulate your business idea, market potential, and how you plan to make it a success.

Market Entry and Growth Strategies

- Market Analysis: Conduct thorough market research to understand your target market deeply. This includes identifying customer pain points, market size, trends, and competition.

- Growth Strategy Development: Plan strategies for market entry and growth. This may involve deciding on marketing tactics, sales strategies, and scaling the business.

Conclusion

Embarking on an entrepreneurial venture is the epitome of taking control of your career. It's a path filled with risks but also potential for significant rewards. As an entrepreneur, you have the opportunity to build something from the ground up, using your sales experience to guide your business decisions and strategies.

In this role, you will wear many hats and face numerous challenges, but the experience you have gained in sales – understanding customers, dealing with rejection, negotiating deals, and more – will be invaluable. Entrepreneurship allows you to channel your passion, creativity, and drive into building a business that reflects your vision and values.

Remember, the journey of entrepreneurship is a marathon, not a sprint. It requires patience, resilience, and a willingness to learn and adapt. If you are driven by the challenge of creating and growing your own business, this path can offer an exciting, profitable, and dynamic career experience.

7.11 Customer Relationship Management (CRM) Specialist

After gaining substantial experience in sales, transitioning to a CRM Specialist role can be a strategic career move. This role focuses on managing and optimizing the CRM system, a vital tool in modern sales processes, ensuring that it effectively supports the sales team's activities and objectives.

Understanding CRM Systems

- CRM Role Overview: A CRM Specialist is responsible for managing the CRM system, ensuring it meets the sales team's needs, and aligning it with the overall sales strategy.

- System Customization and Integration: Customize the CRM system to fit the unique processes and workflows of the sales team. This might involve integrating the CRM with other tools and platforms used by the company.

Data Management and Analysis

- Data Quality Management: Ensure that the data entered into the CRM is accurate and up-to-date. This is crucial for effective sales tracking and analysis.

- Analyzing Sales Data: Use CRM data to generate insights into sales performance, customer behavior, and market trends. These insights are vital for strategic decision-making in sales.

Training and Support

- Training Sales Team: Train the sales team on how to effectively use the CRM system. This includes creating user guides, conducting training sessions, and providing ongoing support.

- Feedback Collection and System Improvement: Regularly collect feedback from the sales team on the CRM system's functionality and usability, and make continuous improvements.

Skills Development for CRM Specialists

- Technical Skills: Develop strong technical skills related to CRM software. This includes understanding software configuration, database management, and basic coding, if necessary.

- Communication Skills: Enhance your ability to communicate technical information in a clear and user-friendly manner. This is important for training and supporting non-technical sales staff.

Conclusion

Transitioning into a CRM Specialist role allows you to leverage your sales experience in a technology-focused capacity. In this role, you become the bridge between the sales team and the technology that supports their work.

Your deep understanding of sales processes and challenges enables you to customize and manage the CRM system effectively, ensuring it provides maximum value to the sales team. As a CRM Specialist, your work directly impacts the efficiency and effectiveness of the sales operations, making you a key player in the organization's overall sales strategy. This role is ideal for those who have an affinity for technology and a desire to optimize sales processes through effective CRM management.

Embracing this role means taking on the responsibility of ensuring that the sales team has the best tools at their disposal to manage customer relationships and drive sales. It's a path that combines technical know-how with a deep understanding of sales dynamics, offering a unique and influential position within the sales ecosystem. With the right approach and commitment to continuous learning and improvement, a career as a CRM Specialist can be highly rewarding, offering the satisfaction of directly enhancing sales performance and contributing to the strategic success of the sales organization.

7.12 Sales Enablement as a Career Path

For sales professionals looking to expand their role in supporting and enhancing the effectiveness of sales teams, a career in sales enablement offers a unique opportunity. Sales enablement focuses on providing the sales team with the tools, resources, and training they need to be successful.

Role Overview and Responsibilities

- Defining Sales Enablement: Understanding the scope of sales enablement, which includes strategizing and implementing processes and tools that help sales teams sell more effectively.

- Content and Resource Development: Creating or curating sales content, like presentations, case studies, and sales scripts that assist the sales team in their selling process.

- Sales Training and Coaching: Developing and delivering training programs that enhance the sales team's skills and knowledge.

Strategies for Sales Enablement

- Aligning with Sales Goals: Ensure that all enablement strategies and tools align with the overall sales goals and objectives of the organization.

- Analyzing Sales Performance: Regularly review sales performance data to identify areas where the sales team can improve and how enablement can assist.

Tools and Technology

- Leveraging Technology: Familiarize yourself with and implement the latest sales enablement technologies, like CRM platforms, sales automation tools, and e-learning software.

- Integrating Tools with Sales Processes: Work closely with the sales and IT teams to ensure that sales enablement tools are seamlessly integrated into the existing sales processes.

Skills Development for Sales Enablement

- Communication and Collaboration: Develop strong communication skills to effectively liaise between sales teams and other departments. Collaboration is key to understanding and addressing the specific needs of salespeople.

- Project Management: Enhance project management skills, as sales enablement often involves overseeing multiple initiatives and resources.

- Analytical Skills: Cultivate the ability to analyze sales trends and performance metrics. This helps in creating targeted enablement strategies that address specific gaps or opportunities.

Conclusion

A career in sales enablement is an exciting path for those who are passionate about empowering sales teams and optimizing sales processes. In this role, you are pivotal in ensuring that the sales team has access to the right tools, resources, and training needed to succeed.

Your contribution as a sales enablement professional directly impacts the efficiency and effectiveness of the sales operations, making you a crucial asset to the organization. This role requires a blend of strategic thinking, content development, technology savvy, and a thorough understanding of sales dynamics.

By embracing a career in sales enablement, you open doors to innovative ways of enhancing sales performance, contributing significantly to the overall success of the sales team and the organization. With a focus on continuous improvement and adaptation to the evolving needs of sales professionals, a career in sales enablement can be deeply rewarding and professionally satisfying.

7.13 Conclusion: Charting Your Future in Sales

As you stand at the crossroads of your sales career, contemplating the next steps and potential transitions, it is essential to take a moment to reflect and chart a deliberate course forward. The journey in sales is as diverse as it is rewarding, offering multiple paths that can lead to professional growth and personal fulfillment.

Evaluating Personal Strengths and Interests

- Begin by conducting a thorough self-assessment of your skills, strengths, and weaknesses. Reflect on what aspects of your sales career you have enjoyed the most and which skills you have excelled in. Are you drawn more to the strategic aspects, the interpersonal relationships, or the thrill of closing a deal?

- Consider your career aspirations. What does success look like to you in the next five, ten, or fifteen years? Aligning your career path with your personal values and interests is key to finding long-term satisfaction and success in your chosen field.

Seeking Mentorship and Guidance

- The value of mentorship in proactively managing your sales career cannot be overstated. Seek out mentors who have walked the paths you are considering. Their insights and advice can be invaluable in helping you make informed decisions.

- A mentor can offer not just guidance on career choices but also on skill development, networking opportunities, and besting the challenges of transitioning to a new role.

Continuous Learning and Adaptation

- The sales landscape is constantly evolving, with new technologies, methodologies, and customer expectations. Embrace a mindset of lifelong learning to stay relevant and competitive. This could involve formal education, workshops, online courses, or self-study.

- Be adaptable and open to change. The ability to pivot and embrace new opportunities is a crucial skill in today's dynamic sales environment. This might mean stepping out of your comfort zone or taking calculated risks to advance your career.

Conclusion

As you contemplate your future in sales, remember that your career path is uniquely yours to shape. It's a journey that intertwines your personal strengths, interests, and aspirations with the opportunities and challenges of the sales profession. By thoughtfully evaluating your skills and interests, actively seeking mentorship, and committing to continuous learning and adaptation, you set the stage for a great career.

Your journey in sales is not just about the roles you take on or the titles you achieve; it's about the experiences you gain, the relationships you build, and the growth you experience both professionally and personally. Each step you take should align with your broader career vision, contributing to a narrative of success and satisfaction that is uniquely your own.

Embrace the journey ahead with confidence and curiosity. With the right mindset, a willingness to learn, and a commitment to personal development, your career in sales can be a rich and rewarding adventure that not only meets your professional goals but also resonates with your personal values and aspirations.

Chapter 8 Conclusion: Charting Your Path in the World of Sales

As we draw this guide to a close, it's clear that forging a successful career in B2B sales is both an art and a science. It requires a blend of innate talents, learned skills, and a mindset geared towards continuous growth and adaptation. The journey through the world of sales is unique for each individual, marked by its own set of challenges, triumphs, and learning experiences.

Embracing the Core Elements of Sales Success At the heart of a thriving sales career lie the fundamental elements we've explored: emotional intelligence and self-awareness, business acumen, and the ability to manage complex projects and navigate digital marketing landscapes. These are the pillars upon which you can build a robust career. They allow you to connect deeply with clients, understand the intricacies of the market, and stay agile in an ever-evolving industry.

Cultivating the Right Attitude and Approach Your attitude in sales is just as crucial as your skills. Cultivating traits like curiosity, determination, persistence, and resilience will not only enhance your performance but also enrich your experience in the field. These traits are your armour and tools as you navigate the highs and lows of a sales career. They will help you bounce back from setbacks, seize opportunities, and stay motivated through it all.

Avoiding Pitfalls and Steering Your Career We've delved into the common pitfalls that can sidetrack your career and how to steer clear of them. Remember, being aware of these potential missteps - from mismanaging your personal brand to staying too long in a comfort zone - is half the battle won. Proactive career management, setting clear goals, and regular self-assessment are vital practices that will keep you on the right track.

Financial Aspirations and Personal Growth
Balancing your financial goals with your personal and professional growth is crucial. It's about setting realistic financial targets and aligning them with your career path, all while ensuring they resonate with your personal values and aspirations. This balance is key to not just professional success but personal fulfilment.

The Journey is Yours As you stand at the precipice of your career in sales, or perhaps as you seek to elevate it to new heights, remember that this journey is inherently personal. Each challenge you face, each success you celebrate, and each lesson you learn adds to the richness of your unique career path. Embrace each experience with an open heart and a willing mind.

A Final Word Let this book be a compass as you navigate your sales career, but remember, the true guide lies within you - in your passion, your dedication, and your willingness to grow. The world of sales is dynamic and challenging, but it is also incredibly rewarding. It offers a platform to not just achieve professional success but to also forge meaningful relationships and make a tangible impact.

As you close this chapter and embark on your journey, carry with you the lessons, strategies, and insights you've gained. Approach each day with a learner's mindset, a warrior's spirit, and a victor's resolve. Your path in sales is not just about the destinations you reach but the journey you undertake to get there. Embrace it, thrive in it, and let it be a journey that reflects not just your professional acumen but also the depth of your character and the height of your aspirations.

Go forth and conquer! Chart your own unique path in your sales career, and may it be as rewarding as it is successful!

Finally, I'd love to hear from you! Please let me know how this book has helped, or if you have any feedback or questions.

Additionally, if you're interested in one-to-one virtual coaching just drop me a line to discuss.

Johnathan Pascall

salescareersunveiled@gmail.com

Appendix. Basic Sales Terminology (Jargon) to Help you Get Hired and Make the Best Impression When You Start your Job

By understanding these terms, a young sales professional can navigate their first role and interviews with confidence, demonstrating a foundational knowledge of essential sales concepts and practices, and not getting lost or confused by sales jargon.

Account: In sales, an account refers to a customer or a potential customer that is managed by a salesperson or a sales team. An account typically represents a business or an organisation (rather than an individual consumer) and may include all the ongoing transactions, communications, and business relationships with that particular client.

Bids and Tenders: Bids and tenders are formal offers made by a supplier to provide goods or services at a specified price. They are often part of a competitive process (tendering) where different suppliers submit bids based on an RFP.

Business Case: A detailed argument, usually in a documented form, that outlines the benefits, costs, and impact of a proposed sales project or decision.

Business Plan: A comprehensive plan that outlines objectives, strategies, sales targets, and detailed plans for reaching these targets in a business.

Buying Persona: A semi-fictional representation of your ideal customer based on market research and real data about your existing customers, including behaviors, motivations, and goals.

Call Plan: A strategy or a plan of action designed for conducting sales calls, including objectives, key messages, and desired outcomes for each call.

Case Studies: Documented examples of how a company successfully helped its customers. In sales, these are used to demonstrate the value and effectiveness of a product or service.

CRM System (Customer Relationship Management System): A technology system that helps manage all your company's relationships and interactions with potential and current customers.

Demand Creation: The process of driving awareness and interest in a company's products or services, often through marketing and sales efforts.

Discovery: The phase in the sales process where you gather information about a prospect's needs, challenges, and goals, typically through asking questions.

Forecasting: The process of predicting future sales performance based on historical data, market analysis, and sales trends.

KPI's (Key Performance Indicators): Measurable values that demonstrate how effectively a company or individual is achieving key business objectives.

Lead: In sales, a lead refers to an individual or organization that has shown interest in a product or service and may potentially become a customer. Leads are often the first point of contact in the sales process, identified through various channels such as marketing campaigns, trade shows, referrals, or direct inquiries. They are considered prospects for sales but require further qualification to determine their likelihood of making a purchase.

Messaging: The key ideas and language a company uses to communicate its value proposition and benefits of its products or services to the target market.

MQL (Marketing Qualified Lead): An MQL is a lead that has been deemed more likely to become a customer compared to other leads, based on specific criteria and actions. These criteria are usually defined by marketing efforts, such as interacting with marketing content, visiting the company website, or downloading resources. MQLs are not yet ready for direct sales outreach but are nurtured through marketing processes. See also Qualification.

Multi-Threading: A sales strategy that involves engaging with multiple contacts or stakeholders within a prospective client's organization to build broader support and understanding.

Next Steps: The actions to be taken after a sales meeting or interaction, usually agreed upon by both the salesperson and the prospect.

OKR's (Objectives and Key Results): A goal-setting framework used to define and track objectives and their outcomes.

On Target Earnings (OTE): The total expected income a salesperson can earn if they meet all their sales targets, including both base salary and commission.

OEM (Original Equipment Manufacturer): An OEM is a company that produces parts or equipment that may be marketed by another manufacturer. For example, a company that makes processors for computers can be an OEM.

Pipeline: A visual representation of where prospects are in the sales process, from initial contact to closing the deal.

Pipeline Generation: The process of creating new potential sales opportunities to fill the sales pipeline.

Positioning: How a product or service is presented or positioned in the market relative to competitors, often highlighting unique features or benefits.

Prospect: A prospect in B2B sales is a potential customer who has been identified as someone who could benefit from the product or service being sold. They have not yet made a purchase but have been qualified as a likely buyer.

Prospecting: Prospecting is the process of searching for potential customers or clients to generate new business. It involves identifying potential prospects and initiating contact with them.

Qualification: Qualification is a process in sales where a lead's likelihood to buy is assessed. This involves determining whether the lead has a genuine need for the product or service, the authority and budget to make the purchase, and a timeline for buying. Sales qualification helps prioritize leads that are more likely to convert into customers, ensuring sales efforts are focused effectively. See also MQL & SQL.

Quota: A sales target set for a salesperson or team to achieve in a specific time frame, often used to measure performance.

Reseller: A reseller is a company or individual that purchases products from manufacturers or wholesalers and then sells them to their customers. In B2B sales, resellers are important partners who help extend the reach of products to different markets or customer segments.

Return on Investment (ROI): A measure used to evaluate the efficiency or profitability of an investment, calculated as net profit divided by the cost of the investment. A key part of a good business case.

Request for Information (RFI): An RFI is a preliminary document a company issues to gather general information from potential suppliers. Unlike an RFP, it's not focused on receiving a bid or proposal but rather on collecting information to understand the offerings in the market.

Request for Proposal (RFP): An RFP is a document issued by a business or organization when they want suppliers to bid on providing a product or service. It outlines the bidding process and contract terms and provides guidance on how the bid should be formatted and presented.

Sales Demo: A sales demo or demonstration is a presentation by a salesperson or pre-sales consultant to show how a product or service works. It's designed to illustrate the product's features, benefits, and suitability to meet the prospective customer's needs.

Sales Cycle: The sales cycle refers to the total time (usually measured in months) it takes to close a sale. that starts from the initial contact with a potential customer (prospect) to the finalization of a sale.

Sales Enablement: The process, tools, and technologies that empower sales teams to sell more effectively. In mid-market and upwards, companies will often have a dedicated Sales Enablement department

Sales Methodology: A framework or set of principles that guides how a salesperson approaches each phase of the sales process. Examples include: Solution Selling, MEDDICC, SPIN Selling, The Challenger Sale (all available as books on Amazon).

Sales Operations: This term refers to the set of activities and processes that support and enhance the efficiency and effectiveness of a sales team. Sales operations include tasks like managing sales data and analytics, overseeing sales tools and technology, implementing sales strategies, and handling administrative functions that enable the sales team to focus more on selling and less on operational tasks.

Sales Opportunity: A qualified lead or prospect that has been identified as having the potential to make a purchase.

Sales Playbook: A sales playbook is a document or set of guidelines that outlines a company's sales process, best practices, strategies, and tactics. It serves as a reference for salespeople to understand the most effective ways to engage customers and close sales.

Sales Process: The series of steps a salesperson follows to move a potential buyer from initial contact to closing the sale.

Sales Stages: Sales stages are the specific steps in a sales cycle that a salesperson follows to move a prospect from initial contact to closing the sale. Common stages include prospecting, qualification, proposal, negotiation, and closing.

SQL (Sales Qualified Lead): An SQL is a lead that has been evaluated by the sales team and deemed ready for direct sales engagement. This determination is based on further qualification criteria, such as the lead's fit with the product or service, their decision-making power, and their interest level. SQLs have passed the initial marketing qualification stages and are considered ready for a more direct sales approach. See also Qualification.

Stakeholders: Individuals or groups who have an interest in or are affected by the outcome of a sales process, including customers, team members, and company leadership.

Targets: Specific, measurable goals set for a salesperson or team to achieve, typically relating to sales volume, revenue, or customer acquisition.

Territory: A specific geographical area or segment of customers assigned to a salesperson or team, for which they are responsible for all sales activities.

Territory Management: The process of strategically planning and managing a salesperson's activities within their assigned territory to maximize sales efficiency and effectiveness.

Use Cases: Specific examples or scenarios that demonstrate how a product or service can be used to solve a customer's problem or improve their situation.

Value Proposition: A value proposition is a statement that clearly explains how a product or service solves customers' problems or improves their situation, delivers specific benefits, and tells the ideal customer why they should buy from you and not from the competition.